Bethlehem Ghosts

Historical Hauntings
In & Around
Pennsylvania's Christmas City

By
Katherine Ramsland
and Dana DeVito

Second Chance Publications
Gettysburg, PA 17325

Published by SECOND CHANCE PUBLICATIONS
P.O. Box 3126
Gettysburg, PA. 17325

ISBN-13: 978-0-9752836-2-2
ISBN-10: 0-9752836-2-6

Cover art by Thomas Staub: haunted@rogers.com
Photos by the authors unless otherwise credited.

TABLE OF CONTENTS

ACKNOWLEDGMENTS

It's not possible to write a book of this nature without assistance from people who are willing to tell the tales, either what they'd heard or what they'd experienced. So we have a number of people to thank for making this collection possible. We'd like to acknowledge the help of the following people: Carolyn Bernhard, Becky Bartlett, Shirlee Neumeyer, Ruth Whitmann-Price, Deb Gruber, Kenny, Robbie, and Shannon at Braveheart, the staff at the Limeport and Newberg Inns, George Motter, Alicia Rambo, Reverend Chuck Holm, Reverend Gary Piatt, Melanie Gold, Natalie Boch, Donata Kelly, Mitzi Flyte, Lisa Higgins, Colleen Lavdar, Blair Murphy, Joanne Smida, Steve Steward, Patty Wilson, Kurt Laudenslager, Gail Priestas, Charles Erb, Bill Carmody, Al and Maria Stempo, Neville Gardner, Larry Fox, John Timpane, Henry Johnston, Donna Johnston, and members of the Greater Lehigh Valley Writers Group.

We're grateful to all the Lehigh Valley historians mentioned and to Adi-Kent Thomas Jeffrey for alerting us to several Bucks County tales; as well, to Charles Adams for the digging he did in this area for *Ghost Stories of the Lehigh Valley*.

Dana: I want to thank my three sons, who provided me with my first ghost experience. I love you all.

Katherine: Special thanks from me to Rick Fisher, and Mark and Carol Nesbitt, who have been a significant part of my ghost expeditions since I wrote *Ghost*. Rick has always been willing to teach me things, and Mark and Carol are among my most cherished friends. They were gracious enough to encourage us to pen this book for publication.

INTRODUCTION TO GHOSTING

Directly across Route 378 from Main Street, some ways down First Avenue from West Broad Street in West Bethlehem, is an inconspicuous memorial that marks a burial ground. It's for the Continental Army, 1777–78, specifically, for the Unknown Soldier. When I went to see it, I read the plaque and then looked up at the cars rushing by just over the edge on the four-lane highway below. Those people were probably driving obliviously over graves more than two centuries old, crushed beneath layers of packed dirt and macadam. In fact, only a decade ago, some remains were unearthed very close to this spot.

War Memorial

In February 1996, a building contractor installing a retaining wall dug up a human skull in the side yard of a First Avenue home. Then another skull was unearthed, along with scraps of wood and iron nails dating back 200 years. More digging ensued, this time by archaeologists, who found evidence of three sets of remains, sparking speculation that the area may well have more buried skeletons. No one today knows where the boundaries of the ancient burial ground are located.

On May 26, 1996, the remains of the three former soldiers were buried near their fellow patriot at First Avenue and Market Street, complete with a celebratory parade. But it's likely there are others, as yet undiscovered, lying deep in someone's yard, under houses, streets and sidewalks.

It made me wonder about hitchhiker ghosts. Were there any around here, rising to the surface and hoping to thumb a ride? Or would such spirits be frightened of cars and seek quieter sites?

In fact, there is a famous story about a phantom hitchhiker not far away, in Bucks County, and it is no stretch of the imagination (unless you just don't believe in ghosts) to figure that he could have gotten a ride on some lonely night right into Bethlehem. The first sighting was in Dublin in 1972. A young man with blond hair wearing a brown jacket and carrying a backpack flagged down a driver on Route 313. She ignored him, but saw him twice more that night, many miles from the original spot and always arriving to the next spot before she did—but no one had passed her. He was also seen in New Jersey, New Hope, and even off River Road outside Riegelsville, just a few miles from the border of Northampton County. In 1989, I heard a woman claim that this ghostly manifestation was of her own brother, who was hitching one night and was hit by a truck, but I was never able to verify that story. In any event, it's reported that whenever a driver asked the thumb-rider where he was going, he'd vanish.

That is a common story where ghosts are concerned, from Jersey to California. Either they don't like answering questions, or it takes so much energy to conjure up a reply that they lose their grip and dissolve.

WHAT ARE THEY?

"We arrange ghosts to haunt us where we can never be."

A friend of mine, John Timpane, sent me this line once from one of his poems. I thought it profoundly captured just why we find ghosts so intriguing. They concern a part of ourselves about which there is an abiding mystery. To some extent, they're about our invisible souls, specifically whether or not our souls possess more enduring substance than our bodies. We want the mystery solved, so we embrace it through ghostly lore, but in some ways we don't really want it solved at all: it's more interesting to keep chasing ghosts. In fact, we like to be scared, in a contained sort of way. Ghost stories provide that container.

While this book is primarily about narratives local to the Lehigh Valley, inspired by what we've heard on Main Street and its surrounds, I will mention other stories I've encountered that illuminate some aspect of ghost lore or ghost hunting. I'll generally tell this book in first-person, because it's easier, and whenever my co-author and co-ghoster accompanied me (or agreed with me), I'll revert to "we," but I'll make it clear when my responses to a situation are mine alone. I'm not really a ghost hunter, nor am I an exorcist, although I've participated in both experiences. I've collected ghost stories on my travels through dozens of countries and every state in the U.S., and I'm always amazed by how similar they are from one culture to the next.

Dana DeVito, who manages the Moravian Book Shop, enjoys ghost stories as much as I do. We have been out together on several occasions, equipped with cameras and recorders, hoping to collect something awesome.

"I have always been interested in ghosts and ghost stories," Dana says. "My favorite books as a child, and even now, are the ones that make me want to sleep with the light on. Mysteries and stories of the supernatural and unexplained were always intriguing. This is how I met Katherine. She came into my store one afternoon to introduce herself as new to the area, and to discuss an event for her new book, *Ghost*. We talked about her experiences. I then asked quite boldly if she ever took anyone 'ghosting' with her. She explained that normally she did not but that she would take me. Now how could I pass that up? Thus began our friendship, and to my delight, my best friend can be just as gruesome as I—no easy task."

Dana had already told me a story from the area that is one of her favorites:

On Montgomery Street in Bethlehem sits an elegant two-story, cape-style home. The house has a stairway to the second floor that divides it into two separate sections. To the left is a bedroom, belonging to the eldest son, "Alex," that runs from the front of the house to the back. At the top of the stairs is the bathroom, and directly across from Alex's room is another bedroom occupied by his two younger brothers, "Matt" and "Scott." (Names changed to protect their identities.)

One morning, Alex, known to sleep-walk, questioned his mother about a screaming man in a black cape and tall black hat who'd run by his bed in the middle of the night and disappeared into the closet. How could someone have been in their house, he asked, and behaved in such a manner? His mother, used to Alex's night wanderings and active imagination, reassured him that no one by that description had been in the house the previous night. She suggested he was quite possibly dreaming. Alex said nothing more, not even telling his brothers.

Several weeks later, the youngest brother, Scott, reported this experience one morning. He had gotten out of bed to use the facilities. As he walked into the hallway, he glanced toward Alex's room and in the doorway he saw a man wearing a dark cloak and a tall, dark, witch-type hat. Scott quickly retreated to his bed, choosing discomfort for the remainder of the night over an encounter with that man.

His mother, puzzled, assured him it was his imagination. She figured Alex had told him and he'd had a dream. Not wanting to face being teased by his brothers, Scott kept the incident to himself.

Several more weeks passed, and when the family was having dinner one night, Matt, the middle child, described his encounter with the same apparition. He'd woken up one night that week for no particular reason. Because his bed was situated by the door, he could see directly into Alex's room. There he saw a cloaked figure, dressed in black and wearing an "Abe Lincoln" hat.

Well, this made for a lively conversation at the table, as the other two boys recounted their experiences. Except for a slight variation or interpretation of what the hat looked like, the figure seen by each boy was essentially the same. No one knew who it could have been, but it was disturbing. They concluded that the house was haunted.

Thereafter, the family saw the same figure many more times, always in Alex's room, and since it seemed to intend no harm, they began to refer to him affectionately as the Top Hat ghost.

THE ART OF GHOSTING

Since I introduced Dana to ghosting, I'll begin our book with some background on what it's about and how we became partners in this venture. I coined the term, "ghosting," in *Ghost: Investigating the Other Side*, to describe the many activities surrounding the idea of a ghost. There are people who merely collect the lore, locally, nationally, or internationally, while others strive to actually spot or photograph a ghost. This is usually referred to as "ghost hunting." They might also seek to record ghostly voices, research the story behind a haunting, or ask a psychic to give them some insight. Perhaps they'll have a séance to try to communicate. Or they might believe that the ghosts must be freed or exorcised—ghost busting—so they will do things such as burn sage or ask a priest or medium to cleanse the place. All of these activities come under the idea of ghosting. But for us, it's mostly about documenting actual events related to what we've heard about or recorded.

Well-equipped ghost hunters these days rely largely on digital technology. They will typically have a digital camera, a video recorder with infrared lighting (or an infrared filter) for recording in the dark, night-vision goggles or binoculars, meters that record various energy signals (heat, movement, and electromagnetic energy), and voice recorders (digital or tape). If they're quite sophisticated, they might adapt other tools to assist in facilitating camera shots (such as a plumber's snake equipped with a camera), and they will be familiar with computer software that enhances photographs and recordings. (Personally, I found it difficult to trudge around with all this equipment, so my own preference is a digital recorder, a video camera, and a small digital still camera. I leave the meters to others who want to document and experiment.)

The first ghosting expedition on which Dana accompanied me took us after dark into Nisky Hill Cemetery, which stretches for several blocks along East Church Street and is the location of a rather infamous monument that resembles a certain body part. The records go back to 1849, when the plots were first laid out, and it's one of the largest older cemeteries close to the downtown Bethlehem area. You can easily walk to it from Main Street. The first burials were Moravian, starting in

1864, but it has since become nondenominational. I know of no particular ghost story associated with this cemetery, but I've heard of a suicide carried out within its gates. But that happened after our expedition.

Nisky Hill Cemetery

I'd already told Dana that the five basic types of manifestations on photos are: bright round images referred to as "orbs" (usually white); a string of those, which form a vortex; a long, electrical snake-like image (I don't know a name for it); foggy stuff that we call ectoplasm (for what it's worth); and the rare but exciting apparition. This latter can be in the form of a single body part, such as a hand, a head or pair of legs, or it can be the entire image of a person. As such, it might be transparent, solid white, or in full color—like the hitchhiker (people even reported his blue eyes). We were most likely to get an orb, I told Dana, though I had sometimes gotten vortexes and "ecto." I had personally never photographed or videotaped an apparition …yet.

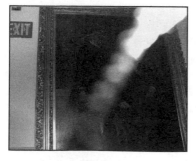

Example of a Vortex   *Orb in Motion*

We had my usual tools, although Dana's digital camera refused to work. I let her use mine. We walked along, looking for a likely spot, and I figured that the walls of mausoleums make the best backdrop, especially if there are street lights around (which diffuse the infrared and digital effects). At first, we didn't get any ghostly results, but then Dana got a picture with a very clear, bright round orb. She was happy. We didn't stay long after that because we encountered a bat crawling around on the ground, and thinking it might be sick, we scooted out. But at least Dana had been initiated.

We've gone ghosting several more times since then, although we've stopped short of actually trying to chase a ghost out of a place. We don't mind that they are there and prefer to leave them be. I'll tell more about our Bethlehem-based activities in the next part.

So have I ever seen a ghost? I'm not sure. Have I heard, smelled, or touched one? Perhaps, if you count voices caught on tape that weren't heard by the naked ear. Dana and I had one rather singular experience, not in the Valley, but elsewhere in Pennsylvania.

THE MINERS' HOTEL

The Miners' Hotel (Photo Courtesy of Blair Murphy)

There were supposed to be eight of us arriving at this old miner's hotel in Windber, no longer in use, but only four showed up. Blair was the hotel's owner. The son of two funeral directors, he'd purchased the place on eBay for a small sum, and then set about to live in it. He learned about several deaths associated with it, including a fatal fight in the bar and an accidental death on a balcony. After a few creepy incidents that occurred when he was all alone, he asked me to bring some others for a night of ghosting.

Dana was one and Sande, a cadaver dog handler, the other. Blair had also invited a psychic, but she canceled at the last minute, apparently unable to have foreseen when she'd accepted the invitation that she wouldn't actually make it. Then our fifth member was Otter the dog—aka Hairy Otter, because he was a large terrier of some sort, with curly fur hiding the top part of his eyes. We also had a couple of people who wanted to see what we were doing and they became our designated diggers.

It was, appropriately enough, a day of thunderstorms and rain. That made the dark three-story building even darker. We sat in the magnificent old bar for a while, and after we all got acquainted, we took Otter into the cellar to scope out the dirt floor. Blair described rumors of at least one body buried down there, so we had reason to believe the dog would point to the location. Otter showed a mild interest in a few areas, including a corner where the absent psychic had indicated was the likely site of a burial. That was sort of exciting, and we floated on that for the better part of the day, hoping that the diggers, when they came later, would turn something up.

Then we went to the first floor. Nothing. Otter ran around, looking for scents, but gave no indication that he'd come across anything. (Dogs trained for this type of hunting "alert" with a specific stance, and perhaps a bark or whine, when they find the right odor.) Moving on to the second floor, up a tall flight of stairs, Otter ran into the rooms that had once housed immigrant miners who'd tried to learn English and make some money. Blair had names for each room, depending how he'd decorated it, and on occasion, his friends had stayed for a time in one room or another. A few of them had reported odd experiences.

In the Dead Monkey Room, named for the stuffed monkey from the film set of *Medicine Man*, Otter suddenly stopped and stiffened up. He whined a little and alerted on a wall situated between the Dead Monkey Room and the adjacent Cactus Room. We learned from one of the diggers, who'd just arrived, that when he'd lived in the Cactus Room, he'd always been in a bad mood and didn't know why. Once he'd moved out, it had dissipated. He considered the room to have been haunted by some angry entity.

With Blair's blessing, we broke down the wall as Hairy Otter watched intently. We then scooped out some debris, which we tossed to the floor. Otter went right to some hunks of rock, which I thought looked like fire-glazed bone. His reaction made me wonder, but we found no skeletal remains inside the wall as we'd anticipated. Nor did the diggers, who had by now gone to work in the cellar, find anything of interest. This was not turning out to be the ghosting weekend we'd hoped, but we still had time for something to happen.

That night, we did the typical ghost hunting with recorders and cameras, and added some special Native American touches to try to invite the spirits to visit or show themselves. In my opinion, not much happened, although with the video camera we had recorded a few bright round anomalies. We finally wrapped it up around 2:30 A.M. and went to bed. For my part, I was disappointed.

In the morning, we considered leaving right away, but Sande wanted to do a spiritual cleansing ritual on the building, Otter, and anyone else who wanted it. She was still inside, in the bathroom under the staircase to the second floor, while Dana, Blair and I went outside with the dog. We sat on the lawn to await her. Soon we heard Sande yelling something that we couldn't make out.

"What's she doing?" Blair asked.

"It's probably just part of her ritual," I said.

He got to his feet. "I'd like to see it." With that, he went inside and I decided to follow him while Dana stayed with Otter. We strode past the bar to the main hallway.

Sande was halfway up the staircase and Blair asked what she was doing.

She half turned and said, "Katherine wants us upstairs." Then her eyes widened as I came in behind him. "How did you get down there?" she asked.

I shrugged. "What do you mean?"

"You were just upstairs. I heard you."

"No, I wasn't. I've been outside."

"You were upstairs. It was your voice. You yelled, 'Sande, get up here!'"

Blair and I looked at each other. I hadn't said anything, or been upstairs, and we both knew it. In fact, no one was upstairs.

"C'mon you guys," Sande said. "How did you do it?" She insisted we come clean, as if we'd played a prank.

I shook my head. "I sure wish you'd have gone all the way up the steps." I could only wonder what might have happened. There had been no one but her inside the building and yet she had distinctly heard my voice, loud and clear, beckoning her to come up. She was shaken.

I asked her to describe exactly what had happened, step by step, and she said that while she'd been in the bathroom beneath the steps, she'd heard footsteps going up the stairs. She figured it was one of us. Then there came a shuffling sound on the second floor, like someone moving furniture. It was at that moment that she heard me say, quite sharply, "Sande! Sande!"

"What?" she'd shouted back. She'd come to the foot of the steps and asked, "Do you want Otter?" She thought I'd found something and needed the dog.

"I" apparently then said something muffled, followed by, "Get up here!"

She asked again, "Do you want Otter?" (That was the yelling we'd heard from outside.) She heard mumbling, as if from farther away, so she climbed halfway up the steps and shouted my name. That's when Blair came in. And now that she realized we'd not been in the building, she was quite disturbed.

I jumped up the steps past her to look around. I went into the Coyote Room, but saw nothing there. I took some pictures and tried to get some recordings. Nothing. Same deal in the Cactus and Dead Monkey Rooms. I sensed we'd lost an opportunity by interrupting something that had been in progress. Not that

I'd wanted to sacrifice Sande to anything, but if she'd really heard that voice, then it had wanted her to come. Why? And what would have happened? Now we'd probably never know.

We went outside to discuss this, and a neighbor came by with a dress that had once belonged to the woman who'd long owned the hotel and had died there. I got this sudden idea and thought that maybe Sande looked like her. The slender dress certainly seemed to be her size. I urged her to put it on, and to her credit, she did. And it fit perfectly—even to the length, which reached to her ankles. So she put her hair up in the style of olden times, just in case her caller had been from another time period, and we went up the steps to film her in the Dead Monkey Room. Again, to my disappointment, it was not rewarding.

When we were done with that, Sande went to take off the dress and I checked the room again. I noticed a pile of old ledgers and letters sitting on the table, a lot of plaster on the floor (from us), and the stuffed monkey, motionless in a chair. Nothing out of the ordinary. I was the last one out. I made sure the light was off. Everything was quiet.

Outside, where the others had gathered, Sande decided to go look through the window once more, but from the street. Dana, who had missed out on all this commotion, joined her. Suddenly, with a shriek, they came running. They insisted that as they were looking up at the window for the Dead Monkey Room, the curtain had been drawn aside.

We could see into the room," Dana said, "because the light's on."

"No, it's not," I insisted. "It was off when I left."

"Go look!"

Blair went up to see, and I followed him. To our surprise, the ledgers and letters were now scattered across the floor, the light was on, and the curtain had been pulled aside and set in a certain way that defied the explanation that a stray breeze had done it. (The windows on that floor were all shut.) I wasn't certain that the curtain had not already been in that position, so I checked the photos. In those, the curtain hung straight down. So it seemed that, in the moments since I'd left, there had been some activity in this room.

But finally we had to leave. Blair continued to invite other ghost hunters to explore the place, and one of them, Patty Wilson, sent me a recording of a voice that, in light of what we'd experienced, was chilling. When she asked whoever was in the place just where they were, a voice responded, "In the wall." For what it's worth, this little hotel in western Pennsylvania housed a mystery.

Ghost Tales

Among the reasons I believe that there is something to the possibility of a paranormal manifestation, is that many of the stories derive from credible sources —people who aren't trying to prove anything or gain anything, and who aren't even sure they believe what they're saying themselves. I've also heard the same story about a single location told by people who did not know each other. Well, we could attribute this to collective consciousness and free-floating memories, etc., but let's not. That, too, is just an idea that needs proving.

One of the most impressive real-life ghost stories I've ever heard was written by John Fuller in *The Ghost of Flight 401*, out of which a disturbing movie was made. It has good testimonial corroboration from a range of witnesses, and the reports of ghostly activity were made despite the threat of losing one's job or the respect of coworkers. No one involved sought publicity and no one profited. For my money, it's largely credible.

As the story goes, Eastern Airlines Flight 401 went down in the Florida Everglades in December 1972. Everyone on board was killed, including Captain Bob Loft and second officer Dan Repo. Loft died during the rescue operation and Repo about thirty hours later. He'd confessed they'd made a mistake attempting to work on a mechanical problem while the flight lost altitude.

Some of the L-1011 jumbo jet's parts were salvageable, so Eastern decided to use them in other planes. It wasn't long before crew members on those specific flights starting seeing some very strange things. People seemed to appear from out of nowhere, especially in inappropriate places. Crew members who had known the deceased Loft and Repo, claimed that they were among the filmy apparitions. There were even reports of visitations from several of the dead flight attendants.

Some crew members tried to alert Eastern's management to the incidents, but the company ignored the reports. Those in charge wanted to avoid any hint of problems and were dismissive of the possibility of ghosts. Even log sheets that contained the reported sightings turned up missing. Nevertheless, the reports continued, and passengers, too, claimed to see the phantom manifestations of the former crew. They appeared in various parts of the plane, and Loft was sometimes spotted sitting in first class. (An attendant once asked him why his name was not on her passenger list. She got no response, so she asked the captain for help. As soon as he recognized Loft as the man in the seat, the entity vanished.)

Repo was seen the most often. Galley attendants saw his face reflected in the oven door and they claimed that the small space felt unusually cold. One day, some reports said, Repo apparently fixed an oven with an overloaded circuit. When an engineer arrived, the flight attendant told him she'd watched another man take care of it. That couldn't be, said the engineer, since he was the only one assigned to this plane. When the attendant, who had not known Repo, was shown his photo, she identified him as the oven fixer.

The deceased Repo approached crew members who did not realize he was a ghost, until he disappeared in front of them. He was often seen sitting in the cockpit or reflected in a window, and he seemed concerned about safety. One flight inspector said that as he began his routine, Repo appeared near him to assure him that it had already been taken care of. Repo also reportedly warned an engineer about a faulty circuit, which proved to be true, and gave an attendant a heads-up about a fire. Another problem arose in a hydraulic system, also pointed out by the ghost.

Fuller applied all manner of investigative journalism to discover the truth about these incidents, but a natural explanation for the source of the alleged hauntings remained elusive. He interviewed witnesses willing to tell their stories and discovered pages missing from logbooks for flights on which some of the sightings occurred. He was skeptical but open, concluding that something was genuine about this haunting, and his book remains one of the classic descriptions of paranormal phenomena.

That made me curious to see how he would treat another, even more bizarre, ghost story into which he was invited a few years later. This was the start of modern-day, technological ghosting. Typical of Fuller's style, he approached it with cautious curiosity. From an engineer, George Meek, he learned about an uneducated medium named Bill O'Neil who'd had an unusual visitation from NASA scientist, Dr. George Mueller, dead some fourteen years. His ghost reportedly urged O'Neil to design some equipment that would operate at 29 megahertz, so as to facilitate two-way communication between them. Unsure what to do, O'Neil contacted the editor of a paranormal magazine, who put him in touch with Meek.

Meek went to meet O'Neil, and after hearing his extraordinary tale about Mueller, checked out the information that Mueller's supposed ghost had offered thus far (his social security number, his career history, and unlisted phone numbers of colleagues). When it all proved accurate and could not have been gotten by any public source, Meek believed that what the spirit told O'Neil was possible.

Meek then funded O'Neil's efforts to continue to get information from Mueller, and he helped put together a complicated device that would achieve their dreams. It was called Spiricom. They worked with it for several months until finally, on October 27, 1977, a spirit voice came through the machine. It was a real two-way conversation about getting the controls right. Then they got nothing more for quite some time, but by 1980 they had held over twenty hours of extended dialogue. Meek took these results to his colleagues to try to get more such machines made. But they were unsuccessful.

Taken together, the two stories provide a rather startling account by an investigative journalist who feels that he's been witness to something extraordinary. To his mind, the Other Side appeared to be real and accessible via electronic means, but more work needed to be done to convince others.

So that brings us to the pressing question, what exactly is a ghost?

POSSIBILITIES

Without getting too academic, let's just say there are many theories about ghosts, from these manifestations being souls of the dead (most common) to them being mere psychological projections from our minds. I have found that few theories cover all the reported phenomena, such as phantom ships, animals, and even whole scenes appearing and disappearing, but here are some of the most popular notions.

The electrical impulse wave theory involves the idea that people who die suddenly, such as from suicide, murder, or an accident, become ghosts, because they're confused by the jarring change from life to death. During periods of stress, this theory posits, the brain waves grow more active, and it is possible that they produce an image that imprints itself on the atmosphere of a certain place, remaining there, though the person is now gone. Perhaps, as the person was passing on, he or she recalled a better time, such as walking through a garden or looking out a window, and that's the image that transfers. This fits with the reports of ghosts who continue to walk on the same floor or stairs they knew in life, even after the floor has been raised or the stairs dismantled.

Others speak of "time slips," where they find themselves in a completely different place, seeing people around them as ghosts. They often see quite a few, or see buildings and vehicles no longer there—or even in existence.

A common idea is that people who want to see ghosts "feed" energy into the phenomenon and thus make it occur, which amounts to a sort of telepathic psychokinesis, particularly if they can make an object move or a door open by itself. In fact, in 1972 a group of eight people in Canada, the Toronto New Horizons Research Foundation, had actually produced numerous paranormal incidents after designing a ghost and concentrating collectively on him. They named him Philip; gave him a tragic history as an English aristocrat, and a reason to have returned as a ghost; and listed his likes and dislikes, habits and customs. For some time, nothing happened, but they persisted in trying to get Philip's attention. Eventually, they grew bored with the serious séance approach.

When they stopped concentrating and decided to just have fun and relax, they suddenly got results: raps or "answers" on the table in response to songs and questions, the "answers" being in perfect accord with the invented personality. Then the table began to move and once even shot across the room. They experienced cool breezes and saw metal bending by itself, and captured all of this on film. When one member told "Philip" that they had made him up, the activity ceased. It picked up again when the group resumed "belief" in his existence. One might assume from the results of this experiment, then, that all such phenomena are psychological in nature. But that's too simplistic.

We'll address the "Philip Phenomenon" later in the book, because other groups have tried it as well. It's an important addition, not to be lightly dismissed, but it doesn't explain all paranormal events, either. (And it's possible that their "visitor" might not actually have been their creation.)

If ghosts are not telepathic images, are they spirits or souls of those who have died? Mediums believe that only people who have the gift can contact these spirits and that the spirits often have messages for those left behind, but I have never seen a convincing demonstration of this. Also, there seem to be manifestations that I've come to understand as residual hauntings, in which ghosts repeatedly go through a scenario, such as a murder—which includes ghostly images of people who did not die in that same context. In other words, a haunting of a victim running from a killer will include not only the victim but also the killer—although only one of them actually died in that situation.

Then there's the issue of poltergeists, which arose in some places we investigated. The notion is that some mischievous spirit moves things around, throws items across rooms, hits or pinches people, and otherwise persistently makes life difficult. Most paranormal experts believe that this is an energy manifestation from living people, typically adolescent or preadolescent children. In other words, a poltergeist is not a ghost. But does that mean that no ghostly manifestation might be playful or even aggressive? Not necessarily. They just haven't been given a name that distinguishes them, so "poltergeist" often covers any of a variety of entities or events.

One type I want to discuss is what's referred to as the "shadow people," because many of our sources mentioned this experience. Among the most common types of sightings, it's also the most easily dismissed as a figment of the imagination.

Shadow people manifest as dark forms just beyond one's full field of vision. In general, they are considered to be not quite human because their features, if spotted, are somewhat distorted. As the legend goes, they usually flit out of view so fast it's difficult to know if anything was really there. They can supposedly disintegrate, move through walls, or just shoot away when there's danger that they might be fully seen.

The real question is whether they have some sort of intention toward us. Some people have reported black shadows that were ominous and even hurtful. In fact, I heard such a story in nearby Bucks County. They can be as small as children or larger than humanly possible. The feeling is often that they're just running through. If they raise any feelings, it's usually a chill or sense of dread—and always a feeling of a full-bodied presence.

How the phenomenon of shadow people occurs is anyone's guess, but theories hold that they are the manifestation of a mass of negative energies, often deriving from some traumatic event, or that they are the residual energy of evil people. Perhaps they have nothing to do with human beings and are just entities that share our space for some fleeting period, or perhaps they're the "demons" of religious lore. In addition, they could be merely the random illusions of our perceptual fields, not to mention the effects of certain drugs, alcohol, and a lack of sleep. Whatever they are, people who tell stories about their experiences with ghosts often describe this fleeting "shadow person" phenomenon.

There's much more that can be said about ghosts and ghost hunting, and we'll include some of these ideas along the way. Since this is a book about Bethlehem hauntings, let's go walk down Main Street.

SPIRITS OF BETHLEHEM

CHRISTMAS ECHOES

Around the Lehigh Valley, there was once an unusual form of paranormal activity, said to have occurred twice a year. The story made the rounds years ago, told by women working together on needlecraft, and it derived from an early tradition of the Moravian community.

After the Revolutionary War, the Moravians established a school for girls in Nazareth, where they learned about manners and decorum. A key subject was music, with an emphasis on hymns. At Christmas time, a walking procession started in Nazareth and went to Bethlehem, with literally hundreds of people on the road singing Moravian hymns. The groups were divided into men, women, boys, and girls, each of which sang particular parts. It was a joy to hear all the harmonizing voices. At first, the procession protocol was informal, with leaders starting up the songs and the others joining in. In time, the hymns were arranged into a regular program, so that singers who took part knew what to expect. It was an event to which many people looked forward, and eventually a similar procession was organized during Easter.

Over the years, as more outsiders moved into the community, there was less participation in this ritual and the tradition eventually fell off. Finally, there were no processions at all. But that didn't seem to stop the music. Some swore that at Christmas time, they could still hear the choruses, even when no one was there. It was so real, they would look to see if someone was once again leading a procession. But they saw only the cold night air, and perhaps some snow.

Thus, the tale of the Singing Ghosts was passed around, with special glee that the music the Moravians so cherished continued, even if the processions did not. As one woman put it, "Maybe it's just a special type of echo that has been around for a long, long time."

That is certainly one theory of what a ghost might be.

THE MORAVIANS

Let's start on the southern end of Main Street, with Moravian College. That means learning more about the Moravians, one of three core Germanic cultures in Pennsylvania. They liked plain living and disliked war. Highly educated and disciplined, they valued books and culture, promoting religious music and church ritual as an intrinsic part of their lives. One of the earliest groups to fight for freedom of religion, the Moravians trace their roots to Europe, back to the Bohemian reformer John Hus, who was burned at the stake for his religious beliefs on July 6, 1415. This intimidated his followers and the movement disbanded or went underground.

Four decades later, a number of Hus's followers—"the United Brethren"—came together in the Bohemian mountains to support one another and keep their faith alive. They remained low profile for decades, but worked on their doctrines and music. Their first collection of hymns—comprising the earliest Protestant hymnal—was published in 1501. They managed to successfully evangelize in several countries. By 1517, the church had nearly 200,000 members in Bohemia and Moravia. Then a wave of persecutions set in, nearly destroying them once again. Small groups secretly stoked the fires, and a dozen Moravians took refuge in 1722 with Count Zinzendorf on his Saxony estate.

Zinzendorf, an idealistic nobleman, was attracted to mysticism. His hospitality seemed a dream come true, until 1736, when he was banished for a decade from Saxony as punishment for harboring fanatics and promoting views contrary to Lutheranism. The Moravians were banished with him, but then, unexpectedly, the banishment was revoked. By then the Moravians' attention had turned to America, in the hope of escaping the European persecutions that seemed to erupt at whim. Some set sail, and after a brief stint at establishing a colony in Georgia, thirteen traveled to Pennsylvania, attracted to the Quakers' pacifism and freedom of religion.

George Whitefield invited the Moravians to settle on "the Barony of Nazareth," a five-thousand-acre tract of land near the forks of the Delaware and the Lehigh Rivers. Since that deal was not without its problems, the Moravians shrewdly purchased five hundred acres where the Monocacy River flows into the Lehigh —the present site of Bethlehem. From there, they acquired more land and set up thriving businesses, mostly framed by their religious and communal views. For this reason, the area became a closed community for almost a century. One could reside there and benefit from services only if one was a member of the Moravian faith. Nevertheless, they were otherwise a welcoming people and took seriously Christ's charge to be hospitable. They developed good relationships with the

Native Americans in the area, bringing some into the fold and teaching them a commercial trade. Zinzendorf himself christened the settlement Bethlehem, after his favorite hymn.

Each Moravian was assigned to a "choir," with membership determined by such things as age, gender, marital status, and particular needs. Parents kept infants with them until they were about eighteen months old, then turned them over to a nursery. After the age of four, the sexes were separated into the boys' and girls' choirs, with different choirs for progressive ages. Then there were the Single Brothers and Single Sisters. If they married, they joined a new choir. After they lost a spouse, they'd join the widows' or widowers' choir. The Moravians believed this type of communal living was the most supportive system, and most encouraging of spiritual conversion. The choir dictated every aspect of a person's existence —eating, sleeping, courtship, marriage, worship, and work.

The first Moravian structure to be built here, no longer in existence, was a small log cabin behind what is now the Hotel Bethlehem. The Moravian settlers cleared the site at the end of 1740 and held a Christmas Eve service in the cabin the following year. (Their animals sheltered within its walls as well.) But the building of the Eagle Hotel in 1823 eclipsed it, just as the Eagle yielded to the Hotel Bethlehem in 1920. But we'll get to that later, along with the ghosts.

The most impressive and immediate building at the end of Main Street is the Brethren House, on the Moravian College campus, and it has a reputation of being haunted.

I should state here that nearly every college and university has some tale of a haunting or two. Over the past three decades on Allentown's Cedar Crest campus, for example, stories have circulated among students about a ghost in Butz Hall. At one point, a professor named her Wanda and there are two different stories associated with her presence. One states that Wanda, a maid in the dorm, had been spurned by her lover, so she hanged herself. The other is similar, but it's a student who commits suicide. However, there's no official record of anyone dying in Butz Hall.

The Linderman Library at Lehigh University appears to house a fairly unfriendly older male spirit, supposedly a former janitor, while Muhlenberg College reportedly hosts the ghost of Oscar Bernheim, who willed his house to the college. Over in Center Valley, DeSales University, too, has its ghosts, but we'll get to that in another chapter. Let's concentrate on one of the oldest buildings on Moravian's historic campus.

THE COLLEGE

Founded in 1742 by the followers of Moravian Bishop John Amos Comenius, the college is the sixth oldest such institution in the country, according to its Web site. The abiding philosophy was that education should be available equally to anyone. Today, the college is known not just for its fine academic program, but also its musical and artistic accomplishments.

Divided into two distinct campuses, the structures near the center of downtown Bethlehem are located on what is now called the Priscilla Payne Hurd campus, while the Main Street campus is nearly a mile up Main Street, to the north. Although several buildings on the Main Street campus inspire tales of ghostly manifestations, from young girls to an elderly couple, we're concerned with the most historic campus.

Brethren House

The four-story Brethren House, aka Colonial Hall, was built in 1748 as a residence for single men. Seventy-two men and older boys initially moved in. As the community expanded, wings were added, and one of the duties of its residents was to play trumpets from the gallery whenever someone died. Soon, specific tunes were assigned to the deaths of people in specific choirs (except when an outbreak of dysentery was thought to be cured by prohibiting the viewing of corpses).

During the Revolutionary War, the building twice transformed into a hospital for the Continental Army, and the Brethren temporarily relocated. However, when necessary, they built coffins and dug graves for the dying soldiers.

A most auspicious guest was entertained at the Brethren House in September 1782. General George Washington and two of his adjuncts arrived to the sound of trumpets. In the chapel, a small ceremony commenced and the general took a glass of wine. He and his men stayed overnight, attending a religious service and inspecting several of the buildings, then leaving the following morning.

After the population of single men dwindled, the building housed the Young Ladies Seminary. Today it's the home of the college's music department—as well as storage for some old furniture.

Given such a history, it's no wonder people report seeing ghosts—especially Revolutionary War-era apparitions.

The Brethren House was the second ghosting expedition for Dana and me. We got permission to go inside one rainy evening and set up infrared cameras. We had heard that a nurse from the days when it served as a military hospital is sometimes seen in the halls and practice rooms, and that the attic light goes on by itself on some nights. Images have been seen in the windows, and there's a tale that a janitor once spotted a seemingly wounded man wandering in the basement with bandages on his head and arm. Apparently he disappeared before anyone could find out what he was doing there.

Dana has been around the area longer than I have and she had heard the following: "Often students are there practicing their instruments in the evening and at night. The tales I heard were of footsteps in the stairway, but nobody being out there when they looked. And there were doors closing by themselves and the sound of knocking from within the walls. There was an incident of someone seeing the image of a person behind them in a mirror, although that might be associated with a girls' dorm down the street."

We set up equipment and waited, but didn't get much action on the first or second floors. However, when we set up the camera in the basement, it recorded some shooting bright lights right away. We waited for a while after that and then got some more. An attempt to record voices did not result in anything. We also didn't see any apparitions, but that's a rare occurrence, in any case. We considered that the building definitely had some kind of unusual energy.

Another legend associated with this building involves a network of underground tunnels, which themselves are said to be haunted by spirits that make a lot of noise. Along with an archaeologist, Dr. Tom Crist, Northampton County coroner Zack Lysek, and a security officer, I looked for the alleged entrance to these tunnels. Under the Brethren House we found what could have been construed as an entrance, now sealed off, so we were unable to take the hoped-for trip into the depths. We went to several other buildings in town that were supposedly part of the network, but came up with nothing.

That same day, we chanced upon a reporter for the *Morning Call* newspaper who told us he'd actually investigated all of this for himself a few years back. It turns out that there were a few tunnels that went from the Sun Inn to the river, but they'd been filled in to prevent kids from getting into them. (Given what I've seen of archways and entrances in some of the basements, I think they also ran down at least one side of Main Street as far as the Book Shop.) As for a mysterious network beneath the city, no dice. It was a myth. Whatever the "entrance" was under the Brethren House, it was not to the tunnels. I guess that means the noisy ghosts supposedly inhabiting these tunnels aren't what people think, either.

Linked to this building, but not on Main Street, is the Sisters' House, which was built just prior to the Brethren House. The section facing Church Street was raised in 1744, and at the time, it was meant as a communal house for single brethren. They outgrew it, and the single women and older girls relocated there from the Nazareth area. Today, it's an apartment house, and a woman who lives there invited Dana and me to come investigate the place for ghosts.

We first took pictures in her apartment, but didn't get anything. She thought we should try the hallway or basement, but the hallway had a light, which prohibited infrared recording, so we set up with two cameras in the basement. Since people came in and out of the building upstairs, it was difficult to get complete quiet, but at least it was fairly dark. Over a period of two hours, we recorded some light orb activity, but nothing that intrigued me, so we ended early. Although this resident said she'd heard things in the hallway, there were no traditional ghost stories associated with the place. Just because we didn't get results does not mean it's free of spirits, but unexplained noise is not sufficient reason to accept a claim of a haunting, either. Perhaps someone will set up a more permanent investigation to see if anything's there.

So let's move on to the impressive Moravian Book Shop, which does have a story. Since the Moravians were ambitious with their printeries and book inventories, we'll add a bit of history.

A BOOK-LOVING SPOOK

As the Moravians settled into the Valley, Bishop Augustus Spangenberg mentioned to Samuel Powell, who ran the Bethlehem Inn in 1745, that they should devise a way to handle books so as to facilitate their educational and religious goals. Thus, the inn, located on Bethlehem's South Side, became the primary place for storing books for distribution. Within a decade, it was a "shop" with an impressive inventory, largely imported from Germany and England, and an organized way to keep the accounts. Because the accounts continued through the years without interruption, the present-day Moravian Bookshop, situated on the North Side, dates its origins to 1745. That makes it the world's oldest continuously operating bookstore.

With an attempt in 1856 to transfer the store to Philadelphia, it took only two years to notice the skyrocketing costs and to back off the transfer plan and return the books to Bethlehem. The new address was 37 Broad Street. In addition to books, a pamphlet by Richard Benert tells us that the proprietor also sold homeopathic remedies. A decade later, the Book Shop was relocated to 86 South Main Street, its current location, but in a much smaller space than what we see now. Members of the Church, involved in the operation of printing and book selling, tore the building down so they could erect a larger one, purchasing the adjacent property to the south.

It was bookseller Henry T. Clauder in 1871 who developed a vision for the store that went well beyond its function for the church. He stocked a wide variety of books and book-related supplies, for enjoyment as well as education. He even managed a lending library. His successor broke away from the printing part of the business, establishing the Book Shop as an independent entity in 1900, soon to be renamed the Moravian Book Shop. In 1924, the shop began to sell the Moravian stars for which they're known (interrupted only by WWII).

In 1970, the shop expanded into the buildings at 434 Main Street, including more gifts and collectibles in their offerings. More areas were added in 1983 and 1992, including a deli, gourmet merchandise, and a card shop. Now at over 260 years in existence, one might imagine that the Book Shop staff have a few ghost stories to tell.

Moravian Book Shop

There are twelve different supervisors who each take a turn closing the store at the end of the business day. The closing duties include physically walking through the store, checking for locked doors, turning off lights, and setting all the alarms. One day, this ritual was slightly interrupted.

The Moravian Book Shop includes the Deli Cookshop which serves light fare and gourmet coffees and sweets. The kitchen is behind the deli at the back of the store. The kitchen and deli are closed one hour prior to the rest of the store and this duty falls to the kitchen crew. It's not a part of the closing supervisor's duty to check it again at the end of the day.

"One Autumn evening," says Dana, "one of the supervisors was in the store at day's end. It was dark at closing time and she was walking through the store. The doors were locked, the customers all gone, and the lights were off.

"We have a long hallway at the end of our deli counter that leads to public restrooms and then to the back entrance to the kitchen. During this supervisor's final rounds, she was startled to see a figure in this back hallway. She'd been certain that everyone but her was out of the store. The figure wore a flowing overcoat and seemingly had run down the hall toward the kitchen. Curious and a little nervous, she went down the hall, dark as it was, and approached the kitchen. This room, too, was fairly dark. She didn't see anyone in there, and there weren't many places to hide, but her attention was drawn to the stove. To her surprise, the burners were still on. She quickly turned off the stove and looked around for the figure. No one was there, so she locked up and got out as fast as she could.

"When she told the story to me in the morning, she said she was actually quite grateful for the figure in the hallway. It wasn't her job to check the kitchen and had she not seen it, she wouldn't have gone into that area. In that case, a fire could easily have started. To this day we thank the 'kitchen ghost' for alerting us to potential danger."

One might think that the shop, as old as it is, would contain more than one ghost, so one night when everyone was gone, Dana and I set up cameras and recorders in the cellar. We ran them for well over an hour, to no effect (a good argument against those who say orbs are just dust particles, for surely we'd have picked up a few of those in this storage area). Still, the supervisor did see a figure that vanished, and it did seem to have a mission, as ghosts in our favorite narratives often have. Apparently, it wanted to prevent its "home" from burning down.

According to theories, some ghosts stick around to watch over us, some have unfinished business and want to find someone to do the job, some seek justice, and some apparently don't realize or accept that they're dead. A few just go through the motions of being in the place where they died, showing up especially on anniversaries, and some hitch rides before vanishing. Some communicate while others remain silent. Some manifest as apparitions, some as noises, and some as fragrances. I've gotten interesting voice recordings from various haunted places, male and female, adult and child, including voices that said such things as, "Do you want to know what I know?" and "Who's the girl?"

Okay, let's move up the street.

GHOSTLY ACCOMPANIMENT

At 452 Main Street, Joanne Smida owns and operates the Hand Cut Crystal shop, where she displays some beautiful crystal glasses, bowls and other items. Facing the store, on the left-hand wall, Joanne keeps an array of music boxes. She recalled an evening when she was alone and one of the music boxes started to play on its own. She can't remember the tune, but it stopped on its own as well. She decided it was time to pack up and go home.

It's happened several times, and she's aware that crystal is an energy conductor, so it doesn't surprise her, but she knew of no story associated with the building that could give the manifestation some personality. Yet, she says, the activity only happens at night when someone's alone; never when customers are in the store during daylight hours. The possibility of a ghostly presence doesn't upset her.

"Music boxes are fun," Joanne says. "People enjoy them, so I think it's a good energy, whatever it is."

Hand Cut Crystal Shop

Perhaps it's a visitation from another building, just up the street. There's no reason to think that ghosts must remain in one location. If they can go through walls, why can't they go check out the nice music and sparkling crystal?

HISTORIC SOULS

Speaking of stores up the street, I once visited the Celtic shop, Donegal Square, run by Neville Gardner, and we got to talking about ghost stories. He told Dana and me the following—a story he's related many times to friends and interested customers:

"Over the past twelve years since I bought our building at 534 Main Street," he said, "we have had many odd things happen of a supernatural nature. The first really noticeable event occurred the night before we opened our tea room in September 1997. I got a call at 6:00 A.M. from a worker in the kitchen who reported that when she came into the kitchen, she found water coming through the ceiling from the apartment above.

"I got dressed and raced in to check it out. Upstairs, in the unoccupied space above the kitchen, the whole place was saturated, but with no evidence of water running anywhere. The carpets were so wet they squished when I walked on them. The doors and windows were all secure, and there was no logical reason why the place was wet. I went into the bathroom, opened the drawers under the vanity and found them filled to the brim with water. It was really strange. I never did figure out where the water came from and this incident never happened again."

Donegal Square

But there were others. I recall that Neville once told me about finding a tunnel behind the store during renovations, and after opening it, there were several weird incidents.

"Our apartment on the second floor above Donegal Square had a bedroom in which apparently something strange happened on a regular basis. During the night, if a guest was sleeping in that bed, they reported feeling something get into bed beside them. This was apparently a pretty frequent and scary event. Other tenants have told stories as well. One tenant told us that one New Year's Eve in their lounge area, they heard a champagne cork pop and heard violin music. They even smelled cigar smoke, but when they opened the door, nobody was there.

"We believe the activity is due to some energy form lingering in this dimension from something that happened in the past. Perhaps it could be something to do with the Marquis de Lafayette, who was nursed back to health in the location where our building now stands after he sustained an injury during the Revolutionary War. The story goes that the daughter of the property owner took care of him and he may have fallen in love with her. The Marquis returned to France shortly afterwards and perhaps the young woman died with an unquenched passion that resulted in the energy that dwells in the building to this day."

Maybe so. Associated with this store is Granny McCarthy's Tea Room—the one Neville mentioned—just around the corner. Melanie Gold, a freelance writer and historian, filled in more detail:

"Lafayette was a close friend to George Washington, and despite his countrymen's warnings, he came to America to fight in the Revolution. His first battle was at

Brandywine, where he was injured. He was sent to the Sun Inn [in Bethlehem] to recuperate, but finding the accommodations too noisy and displeasing, he was sent [nearby] to the home of George Friedrich Bechtel, superintendent of the Moravian farm, where Bechtel's daughter tended to his wound. Lafayette returned to battle roughly six weeks later. It is rumored that Bechtel's daughter fell in love with the already-married Lafayette during his recovery."

Granny McCarthy's Tea Room

She adds that Neville had told her that when he was renovating the medieval banquet hall above the tea room, strange things were happening in there—doors were closing on their own and items were being moved. He also said that someone reported seeing a female apparition, and he surmised that it could have been the spirit of the Bechtel girl.

THE PLACE TO BE

Strolling up to 564 Main Street, we find the historic Sun Inn, one of the most impressive and least accessible buildings in town. Greeting its first guests in 1760, the place has been a lodging house, restaurant and museum. John Hancock once signed the guest registry, and John Adams lodged there, calling it the "best inn I ever saw." The Continental Congress met there in 1777, and, of course, George Washington once visited. In 1792, a deputation from six Indian nations, involving fifty-one chiefs and warriors, lodged there on their way to Philadelphia to meet with Washington. Today, a living history museum occupies the first floor.

"It is doubtful," wrote William C. Reichel, "whether another house of entertainment in the country can lay claim to having sheltered under its roof so many of the leading patriots, statesmen and military chieftains of the War of American Independence as the time-honored Sun Inn at Bethlehem."

After 1755, the inn also served as a central shelter from Indian attacks. This is where the tunnels originate, leading from the cellar down to the river. People could remain in the tunnels for a while, if need be, and when not in use for protection, the rooms below-ground were used to store food.

Sun Inn

Among the sightings of apparitions that I've heard or read about are British or Hessian soldiers in the basement. There has also been a report of a crying infant, whistling, sudden cold spots, and furniture being moved out of place when the inn is closed during the night. One legend indicates that a Brother Albrecht had hidden valuables somewhere inside and his ghost keeps watch over them.

Across the street is the Woolworth's building, where one of the proprietors of the stores currently occupying the space has stated that sometimes, after the doors are locked, he can hear the sound of numerous customers inside, just as if it's the middle of the day.

LADIES AND GENTS

Not quite on Main Street, but not far down West Broad Street, at #52, is an impressive building with front columns that currently houses a branch of the Wachovia Bank. Said to have been a nightclub during the Depression era known as the Colonnade, some time during the late 1930s, a woman was murdered in the club's basement. Some people say it's haunted, but it was difficult to track down specific stories about a ghost. Maybe she's the one that's been spotted at the local theater just down from this building on the same street.

The Colonnade

The Boyd Theater is one of the more interesting movie theater experiences in the region—and least expensive. It opened on September 1, 1921, according to its Web site, as the Kurtz Theater, featuring silent motion pictures and vaudeville acts. Three years later, it became the Colonial Theater, which lasted a decade. Finally, it became the Boyd in 1934 as part of a small chain out of Philadelphia. Reportedly, the figure of a woman from Victorian times has been spotted here. (Okay, Victorian is not the same as Depression-era, but then again, just because she's wearing a long dress doesn't mean she's a Victorian ghost.)

Boyd Theater

We also heard about a house on nearby High Street, possibly occupied by a ghost who appeared to the homeowner in a dream. She and her husband were renovating the older home and they had recently removed the servant's staircase in the back of the house. In a dream soon thereafter, a man introduced himself to her as "William" and told her he had lived there with another man. He declared that they'd been very happy in the house and added that he wasn't pleased that she'd removed the staircase. She didn't think much about this dream until her husband was digging around in the basement and came across a cement block with the name "William" carved into it, along with another man's name and the year 1888.

COLD SPOTS

If you go the other way down West Broad Street, crossing over Route 378, there's another haunted building, although I was asked not to give out the address. Once a funeral home, it became an office building that also rented out rooms on the upper floors. It seems that a tenant who resided on the third floor for three years had some ghost experiences while living there, as did the tenant before him. Neither knew the other, but both described similar experiences. In fact, several people who worked in the offices told me about distinct cold spots in certain places and the sound of someone walking on the stairs when no one was around. Few of them realized the building had once been used for embalming and holding services for the dead.

With the dead in mind, let's go to one of the most visited cemeteries in the Main Street area.

DEATH'S REPOSE

In some older Moravian documents from the eighteenth century, biographies of people were carefully laid out, and one item bears mentioning. In a book called *The Transformation of Moravian Bethlehem* was a discussion about premonitions of death. Having such an experience seemed to be just as important for a spiritual life as a person's relationship with Christ, and was in fact, part and parcel with it. Apparently, people who were attuned to God were so aware of their spiritual condition that they actually knew when death approached. This premonition would occur before they even grew ill. Babies, too, supposedly possessed this ability, and were said to be especially affectionate with their parents during the days just before they passed. Older children and adults were able to articulate the sensation of future awareness, often by predicting that they would be gone before they turned a certain age, or that they would not see a friend or relative again. Sometimes they would just say they knew they were about to meet their Lord.

And then there were the burials. Special corpse, or pre-burial, houses were reserved for the preparation of bodies. In the winter, bodies might also have to be stored until the frozen ground thawed sufficiently to be loosened with shovels. There's no reason to believe these buildings might be haunted, since people did not die in them or have any particular emotional attachment to them, but they nevertheless retain an atmosphere of dark mystery. That's probably because these days we leave death preparations to professionals and distance ourselves.

I'm no expert on Moravian culture, but it's my understanding that Moravians called all of their cemeteries "God's Acre," not because they laid out only a single acre of land but because they hoped to convey a spirit of being set apart and sanctified. Unafraid of death, and even adopting a welcoming attitude about the transformation into a spiritual eternity, they kept their dead close by.

The first God's Acre was in Saxony in Germany, and that's where the notion originated that the bodies are planted into the ground like seeds, with the souls ready to bloom when Christ came for them. The small cemetery here in Bethlehem was laid out in 1748.

While I personally prefer cemeteries with impressive artistic monuments, I can appreciate the equalizing effect of providing the same type and size of headstone for everyone, with all of them lying flat against the ground. That way, no person could distinguish himself in death above any other. In these cemeteries, sections were designated for the various choirs. Members were buried according to the choir to which they had belonged when they died.

God's Acre

In our particular God's Acre, benches allow visitors to sit and meditate, presumably about their immortal souls. Or, they might look for ghosts.

One afternoon I was with a woman, Pat, who claimed to have psychic abilities. We were strolling together through the cozy fenced burial ground when she stopped and seemed to be staring at something in the cemetery's center. I looked in that direction and saw a few tourists, but nothing that would make me pause like that. Pat stated she could see a young woman standing there, appearing forlorn. I looked again but failed to see her.

"She's dressed like she's from the past, but very plain," Pat said. "She looks about sixteen or seventeen years old. She's trying to talk, but there's something wrong with her throat. She's pointing at it, as if she can't speak."

We walked over to read the headstones. Glancing at the dates of birth and death, and making quick subtractions, we found a young woman, age seventeen, who had died from an illness that involved respiratory problems. Well, was that a good guess or did Pat actually see the spirit of a woman who was showing her what she'd died of? I can't answer that, but it was strange.

Before adding the next story, I should indicate that I've had a few interesting experiences in cemeteries. I recounted the following story in *Ghost: Investigating the Other Side*, and I'm adding it here so the reader will understand the next tale, and others later on.

A few years ago, I met people who use equipment such as digital cameras, motion detectors, temperature scanners, and electromagnetic field detectors to lock on to the position of an otherwise invisible ghost. They frequently went into cemeteries. In fact, several of them offered a theory that cemeteries contain "portals" through which spirits move in and out of our dimension (based on what evidence, I don't know). That means that ghost photography and what they call electronic voice recordings are more likely to capture something "anomalous" in a graveyard. In other words, people looking for ghosts have a better chance here than elsewhere of getting recorded evidence.

I went with Rick Fisher of the Pennsylvania Paranormal Society to one of his favorite country cemeteries near Lancaster. He'd told me about disembodied voices that he'd gotten on tape in various graveyards, one of which had called him by name and another had told him to "get out!" I was curious to see if I might record something like that myself—although I wasn't keen about receiving such an order.

The Lancaster area had experienced a serious drought throughout that summer and on this particular night a major storm was on its way. This is a prime condition, I learned, for surges of electromagnetic activity. Rick had a video camera with infrared capabilities, while I had a digital camera, a small digital recorder, and a thermal scanner. I sat down on the grass while Rick walked into the darkness across the cemetery. I pulled out my recorder, looked around to ensure that there would be no obvious disturbances, and began.

"Does anyone want to communicate?" I asked into the recorder. This was a standard procedure. You invite the spirits to talk. Then I listened closely but heard only the sounds of the chirping crickets. I tried again, asking the same question.

I could see from the blinking red light, activated by noise, that it was recording, but there were noises all around in the supposedly still night air. A car went by down the road and then the crickets chirped again. Lightning shot through the distant western sky, with a slight groan of thunder.

After a few minutes, I turned off the recorder so I could play it back. In great anticipation, I pressed the button.

First I heard my own voice asking the initial question, "Does anyone want to communicate?" Then there were crickets, then the car, and then crickets again. Ten more seconds went by and then came a clear voice on the tape that sounded like a young boy. He simply said, "Yes." This was not Rick's voice or mine, and there was no one else around. I hadn't heard it, but I'd recorded it. This was exciting!

I shivered, sensing that "someone" was quite near, perhaps right behind me, and he wanted to talk. I was about to call Rick over when another voice came on. This one was older and kind of whispery. I could not make out the gender, but the words were clear enough: "Why are you doing this to us?"

A chill shot through me. I looked around. Was he talking to me? Why are we doing what? Recording? Taking pictures? Just being there, disturbing them?

I figured it was time to leave. The storm was getting close and other things were obviously closer. Rick and I packed up the equipment and left just as the rain came crashing down. Apparently, the conditions had been just right, but that voice disturbs me to this day.

So that was an experience of EVP—electronic voice phenomena. Since then, I've learned a lot about it, but have been only moderately successful at getting good recordings. Rick is another story. He's gotten hundreds, probably because he goes out ghosting on a regular basis.

So, let's get back to Bethlehem. About a month after the experience with the psychic in God's Acre, I heard about another interesting incident in this cemetery. A local historian, Natalie Bock, was giving a tour in the section for the women's choir, discussing the manner in which the Moravians treated their dead–especially with regard to African and Native Americans. Rick Fisher was there with his trusty digital recorder, and when he returned that evening to listen, he found that he'd recorded a voice, superimposed over Natalie's. It was a simple request that echoed the whole point of the little burial ground: to be quiet. The voice, clearly that of an adult female, polite but firm, said, "Leave, please." Natalie wasn't keen about it, but having studied the Moravians, she understood.

And speaking of Natalie, she figures prominently in the next haunted place we'll visit: the Historic Hotel Bethlehem.

HAUNTED HALLS

One of the first buildings you see to the left, when you get onto Main Street coming from the south, is the four-story Hotel Bethlehem. I saved this place for last in this chapter because it appears to be one of the most haunted buildings in town. The manifestations are benign, but they do have some provocative origins.

Dana and I met in the lobby one morning with Natalie, who had been busy in the library archives. She's a poised, attractive researcher who's working on a history of the hotel. She eagerly told us about what had been on that land before the Hotel Bethlehem and said she'd been surprised to learn about the tales of ghosts.

Hotel Bethlehem

As I have already mentioned, in 1740–41, the first house was erected and in 1823 it was torn down to make way for the Eagle Hotel, necessary for the town's growing industry. Many visitors came in and out of Bethlehem, and some people even used the hotel as a residence. A century later, the industrialist and president of Bethlehem Steel, Charles M. Schwab, tore that structure down to construct the Hotel Bethlehem, aspiring to build the finest hotel the area had ever seen.

I had already heard that the place had visitations. Melanie Gold told me that the third floor was haunted by a suicide victim who had jumped out a window back in the 1950s or 1960s. "My sister-in-law worked there about five years ago," she said, "and talked about rumors of hauntings, including supplies disappearing and reappearing, as well as the spirit of a little girl who haunts one of the floors."

Among the best stories was the sighting of a female ghost walking through the lobby who appeared to be barefoot. That coincides with a news story that Natalie had dug up about a former hostess at the Eagle, wife of the proprietor, who'd apparently met all her guests barefoot. Lovely. Back then, it was scandalous.

We did know the facts about at least one suicide. A man named Frank Smith had an office on the hotel's third floor. Mr. Smith was involved in a partnership that was associated with Bethlehem Steel. There was an agreement in place between Frank and his partners that each of them would take out a life insurance policy naming the others as beneficiaries. In the event of the death of any one of them, the insurance payout would work as a buy-out of that person's share. Eventually, the partnership had financial difficulties and Smith was worried.

One day, his secretary came in early, as usual, and saw his jacket lying folded over the back of his chair. She didn't think anything of it and went down to have breakfast. He was not in the dining room, but she figured he could be somewhere in town, doing business. She worked for the rest of the morning without seeing him. She had to make a copy of a document, so she went to the restroom where they kept the copy machine. The door was closed, so she knocked. It wasn't locked, so she turned the knob to open it, but the door would not budge. She tried pushing, but it seemed to be hindered by something on the other side, so she called hotel security.

They, too, had a difficult time opening the door, but once they did they realized why: Frank Smith's body was lying against it. Apparently, he had gone into the bathroom and shot himself with a .357 magnum. However, further investigation indicated that he'd shot himself twice—once in the leg and once in the head. It's unusual for suicide victims to shoot twice, although there are cases of it. Smith could have even shot himself in the leg accidentally, or perhaps he thought he'd shoot the leg and die from bleeding out of a major artery, but then decided to end it more quickly. Or, he might have been murdered (some people thought so) and then posed to look like a suicide. In fact, he could have been in that room for hours before he was found. Apparently no one heard the shots. In any event, the incident was ultimately declared a suicide.

Because the policy had a clause that specified no payout for suicide within a specific time frame, and the incident was within that restricted period, the partners, along with Smith's wife, had to go to court to argue that the death had been an accident. They lost. There was no insurance payout for any of the parties. Still, the motivation for suicide was unclear, since Smith had left no note. Maybe he was the one who'd staged it, making it look like murder (by shooting himself twice) so the others could benefit from the policy, apparently he was too depressed to wait out the policy's restriction clause. If he had that in mind, it didn't work.

Supposedly, his ghost wanders that floor, making a variety of noises and possibly a few appearances. Natalie had learned that around midday, one day, a housekeeper had seen the figure of a gentleman in a suit, in the bathroom where Smith had died. He had disappeared right in front of her. Needless to say, this housekeeper probably asked to be transferred to another area, if she continued working at the hotel at all. Later, an auditor saw the distinct reflection of a man in a glass tabletop (I'm not sure of its location), but when he looked up, no one was there.

On this same floor, people have reported the loud crash of weights dropping in the fitness area, when it's locked and no one is found inside. Apparently, this has been a common complaint. In addition, from the street below, the image of a little girl was once seen after hours in the window of this same room.

She might be the same girl seen in a white dress in other areas of the hotel. Natalie linked this seemingly benign apparition with a woman who had lived in the hotel as a child—May Yohé. Born in Bethlehem in 1866, the grandchild of Eagle Hotel owner Caleb Yohé, she became a famous singer, gaining renown for her operatic talents. She toured extensively around Europe, settling in England where she married Lord Henry Francis Hope in 1894. Thus, for a time she sported the famous deep-blue Hope diamond—at least until her divorce. She married again, several times, and appeared in quite a few silent

films, including *The Hope Diamond Mystery*. She died in 1938, nowhere near the Hotel Bethlehem. However, she probably had many positive memories of the hotel where she grew up, because she was a pretty little girl, pampered by her parents and the object of attention from many of the guests. She would even sing for them. So, it is not a stretch to believe that her emotional residue might still be floating around the place. In that case, she's a happy ghost and probably just wants to please others.

Natalie had also learned about the death of an infant boy who'd been mysteriously left at the Eagle in 1870. There was no mention of how he'd died, apart from an illness, but he'd apparently suffered some "haps and mishaps," as the papers reported. He was buried in Nisky Hill Cemetery. Also, in 1871, a guest of the Eagle was found dead in an outhouse following a sudden illness the evening before.

Since the hotel was a residence for some people, and since it's not uncommon for travelers to die somewhere en route, there have been more ordinary deaths in these rooms, too, including that of a young boy. One never knows what might precipitate a haunting. One woman who died there had fallen into an excavation site nearby, on her way to Fountain Hill, and suffered from spinal cord injury before finally succumbing. Then there was the accidental poisoning of a child.

More interesting was another suicide from an earlier era: A proprietor of the Eagle, David Lambert, hanged himself on a rear rafter on September 1, 1884. He was 68 and apparently suffered from depression over the death of one of his sons. It was not his first attempt on his life, but it was certainly his last.

Dating back even earlier, Natalie also described a "Cicerone" who patrolled the streets, prohibiting strangers from wandering around, and ran errands for wealthy girls. Dating back to the Revolutionary War era, he was called Daddy Thomas, and he wore a colonial style hat. Apparently, one of the day engineers saw a figure with just such a headpiece in the hotel's sub-basement.

Willing to explore the supernatural, Natalie met me for drinks one Saturday evening, because I told her that, when looking for ghost stories it's always a good idea to get the bartender's perspective. They hear all the tales—even some inspired by a different kind of "spirit"—and they've often seen or heard things themselves,

38

because they work until few people are there and often close up. This bartender immediately told us to speak with one of the night engineers, Steve Steward, who happened to be coming on at eleven o'clock that very night. Steve certainly had a few tales to tell. Long associated with the hotel, he seemed to have heard it all.

From his basement office, in good humor he described quite a few different manifestations, such as workers being tapped on the shoulder, shadow people flitting through the boiler room, and staff members hearing a woman they couldn't see calling out their names. He also had a tale about the fitness room on the third floor. He'd been walking down the hall near the room one night when he saw the image of a tall woman wearing a sweater and gray pants looking at him through the glass door, from inside the room. He had just locked that door and no one had been in there, but there she was, staring right at him. He decided to just walk away and leave her alone. He didn't want to know. He said he also knew of one engineer who'd refused to do any work at night on the third floor.

During the 1980s, Steve said, kitchen staff had reported seeing a woman in a long black skirt and white blouse and cap—the uniform of a waitress—who simply disappeared before their eyes.

One evening Steve had gone into the Moravian Room. The heat was on, but he experienced a cold spot. When he coughed his breath was frosty. He'd also experienced a carpet sweeper turning on by itself in that room, although it was not plugged in. Supposedly, a man had once hanged himself there, but we think that story derives from the hanging already mentioned from the 1800s, because bodies often get moved in the telling and retelling of a tale. Natalie could find no mention in any records of a hanging in that room—nor of one off the balcony, as some tales depict. Another uncorroborated report has someone jumping off the hotel's roof. Steve didn't know about that, but he found the hotel, with its rich history, to be a viable place for strange incidents. None had ever caused harm. They were just interesting.

So, with all of this information, we prepared for the hotel's first "Rooms with a Boo" weekend in April 2007. I was going to give a talk on Friday night about the ghosting equipment and my experiences, and then stay overnight in a haunted room. Natalie chose 932, which had two different stories associated with it (although it's possible that one or the other occurred in another room).

In one version, a couple claimed to have encountered a man in his underwear who'd said, "You're in my room, please leave," so they did. But at the registration desk, they learned that there was no other guest checked into that room. The other was of a young woman who had stepped out of the shower of the newly-renovated bathroom and saw the reflection of a man in the mirror. He'd walked away from her and disappeared. Startled, she got dressed in a hurry and went down to the desk to report this, but when the staff checked, no one else was in the room.

So that weekend in April, I spent one night in this room—which certainly had a view if not a boo—inviting the ghost to talk to me. Apparently he wasn't around or didn't care, because I got nothing with the infrared video camera or on the voice recorder. I slept well and enjoyed the nice bathroom—even took a shower—without incident or reflection (except mine). I'd kind of wanted the man to show up, but he didn't.

The following day, Rick Fisher arrived with his wife. He gave the main lecture about ghost hunting and then set up his equipment in 932. I moved out and they spent the night. In the morning, Rick was able to play some of the voices he had picked up. Among the most easily understood were the following phrases:

"I love the bathroom."

"Watch out!"

"I locked myself in the closet."

"There is a fight."

"Somebody's looking."

Names such as Tom, Karen, Audrey, and Sally.

I'll admit, I was jealous. I had wanted to get such results, but I'll also admit I do not have the persistence that Rick had to stay up all night and then analyze hours of recordings. Still, I'm determined that next time I'll be more prepared. In fact, two months later, in June, I learned that a guest had signed out of 932 with an unexplained notation, "This room is definitely haunted!"

There was more activity throughout the summer. Different guests have described lights flickering, papers standing upright as if being read by someone, a tap on a shoulder when no one was there, a name repeatedly whispered, and one guest claimed to have seen the apparition of a man before she requested another room. She showed the front desk staff the photo she had taken of this entity, but they didn't think to request a copy. Still, there were witnesses who saw the photo and reported it. This guest wasn't there for a haunted experience and hadn't known about (or wanted) any ghost in her room.

It's time now to move on to other areas and other issues. Dana and I also made the rounds of haunted eating establishments, imbibing the spirits in more ways than one. (Remember what I said about bartenders.) We also had an interesting encounter with a haunted family, which led us to wonder about the source of these spooky events. So, let's move on.

Menu, please.

GHOSTS AS GUESTS

Haunted restaurants, pubs and taverns are found in nearly every historic town. The stories range from unusual noises to vague forms to the truly chilling. One of the most shocking we've heard occurred as the result of a brutal incident during the 1800s at a farmhouse. The hired worker was smitten with the landowner's daughter, but when he was denied her hand in marriage, he massacred the family, including the daughter and the maid. He fled, but was apprehended, and after he was hanged for his evil deed, the citizens skinned him and made wallets and lamp shades. Apparently his ghost (or someone's) still wanders the place—now a restaurant that has changed owners many times—shoving the wait staff, tapping on shoulders, lighting candles after hours, and flicking off appliances just turned on.

While that's a good story, on our tour of this area we found no eating establishment with a tale quite that graphic. However, we certainly did partake at a wealth of places where staff members or owners were willing to reveal what they had seen, heard, or felt.

LIMEPORT INN

One of our first ventures out to collect ghost tales involved the Limeport Inn (or Hotel) on Limeport Pike near Coopersburg. I had been there before and had been shown where some of the activity had occurred. We went into the bar, ordered wine, and waited until it was nearly empty (usually a good procedure if you want the staff to take time to talk). Then we started asking questions.

Once a funeral parlor, this beautiful old building that dates back some 160+ years, was where a little boy had reportedly died. No one was sure about the illness he had or whether he'd died as the result of an accident, but several people have heard the voice of the child calling for his mother from the back upstairs bedroom. Some reports even locate the voice outside the second-floor window. A former owner had a dog, and the dog refused to enter this particular room. In addition to the boy's voice, some people have reported the sound of several voices whispering together.

Limeport Inn

But there is activity downstairs as well. On separate occasions, two waitresses said that out of the corner of their eye (remember the Shadow People) they had seen the image of a person seated in the Green Room. But when each looked more closely, no one was there.

The chef told us that when he'd first started cooking at the Limeport in 2002, he went into the closet on the second floor to fetch something. Although he was alone in the building, he heard a male voice close by. He couldn't make out the words, but it felt very creepy to him. He never found its source. In other instances, he told us, he'd often found things turned on after he'd turned them off. It had happened so often that he had started paying attention and knew that he had turned off the stove, or a light, or an appliance, and yet he would find it on. There was nothing wrong with the electrical system. Someone was around.

Spring Valley Inn

The Spring Valley Inn at 1355 Station Avenue may well have hosted the phantom undertaker who once roamed Lower Saucon (more about him in the next part), but these days, the spirit is more benign—and female. Set in a peaceful and rustic area, with its own trout pond, the inn offers excellent fish and seafood dishes, including my favorite, a smoked trout salad. Kurt and Stephanie Laudenslager own and run it.

I was at the inn one evening after a play in the Shakespeare Festival having wine with a couple of actresses. Offhandedly, I asked our waitress, Gail Priestas, if the inn was haunted, since I'm always looking for stories. She was quick to say yes. In fact, it turned out that she'd seen the apparition herself—a woman wearing a long white dress who appears in the women's restroom. The same figure has been spotted walking from that location through the cloak room into the dining room.

I talked with Kurt, who worked at the restaurant for a decade before buying it, and he said the owner before him witnessed the woman in white. She's a quiet figure, keeping mostly to herself. Even so, the eatery is fairly active with incidents, and not much time passes before someone reports something strange. Patrons will say they've just been touched or caressed on the back, and late at night the radio might come on by itself. Kurt has also had cell phone problems, usually late at night, including finding the phone moved from where he'd placed it.

Spring Valley Inn

"She's always been friendly," he says. "She doesn't throw things across the room or anything like that. She seems curious more than anything else." A previous owner's daughter once came in and showed them a photo of her mother, who apparently resembles the woman in white, but as of yet, no one knows her history. Kurt hopes that one day someone will come in and tell them about her.

NEWBERG INN

The Newburg Inn, on the corner of Route 191 and Newburg Road, is an inviting family restaurant and former lodging place. Dana and I sat at the bar and ordered the delicious spinach and artichoke dip and wine, as we put our questions to some of the staff about spooky incidents. Built in 1750, the restaurant's open-beam construction gives it a casual holiday feel, and over the bar is a ceiling of beautiful stained glass. The building has served as a trading post, hotel, and stagecoach stop. Prominant among the deaths there was a Native American boy who hanged himself. One would expect, with such a long and varied history involving so many different people, that there might be supernatural activity. And there has been.

We learned that the former owner, who went by the name of "Newt," liked to sit most evenings on a particular stool at the bar, over which beautiful stained glass panels provide light. After he died sometime in the 1980s, that particular bar stool, when empty, often moved by itself, as if someone was preparing to leave the bar to be on his way. Several people have witnessed it...and wondered.

One person, who did not wish to be named but who said that she'd been sensitive to paranormal activity since childhood, indicated that things were hopping back in those days. She'd once seen an adult male at the top of the stairs. He was somewhat solid but not so much so that she thought he was just a regular person. He looked more like the outline of a person. Besides, no one was supposed to be up there, but there he was.

BRAVEHEART

Braveheart

Formerly the Hellertown Hotel, the 101-year-old building on Main Street in Hellertown now houses "Braveheart," an authentic Scottish pub that provides food, music and spirits—of more than one kind. When we went there one Friday evening for their special cheese plate, wine, and fish 'n' chips, we learned that there had been several deaths in the building—common to hotels. Not that many years ago, the local coroner had come to remove the corpse of a man who had been dead for three days from a drug overdose.

There's paranormal activity in the cellar and on the upper floors, although no one seems to know why. Robbie, one of the bartenders who arrived from England and moved in upstairs, said that on his first night there he heard loud music. At first he thought it was someone's car radio playing outside, but as he walked around to check, it grew more apparent that this music was coming from somewhere *inside* the building. He knew it shouldn't have been, as nothing was on. Suddenly uninterested in further exploration, lest he find something he didn't want to know about in his abode, he stayed in his room. On another occasion, he plugged in a radio and it started right up, although he hadn't yet turned it on. He tried pressing buttons to turn it off, but it kept playing. Nervous about the possibility that it would continue to play if he pulled the plug, he kept trying to turn it off. Nothing seemed to work, but finally, it just stopped.

Robbie also said that he often hears noises in the building and does not like to stay there by himself. Well, all old buildings make noises, but it was his impression, he said, that he could feel the energy of people walking around. In fact, he'd heard some whispering sounds, like, "Psst." He thought it was another person who lived upstairs, but it wasn't. His own impression is that a female spirit roams the building, although he thinks there could well be more than one entity. Since he stays there at night, he doesn't want to think too hard about it.

Robbie has also had an experience which other people witnessed. On the main floor, on the bar, there's a hinged panel that they lift in order to go behind or in front of the bar. One evening, while several servers were present, this panel apparently slammed down into place by itself. It's a heavy panel, and since no one was near it at the time, understandably, it scared them all.

Another person residing upstairs told Robbie that one night he saw the shadow of what he took to be a person pass by the open door of his room. Believing it to be Robbie, he went to look, but no one was there. Robbie later told him that he hadn't been upstairs at that time. In fact, no one else owned up to it, either.

The manager, Debbie Gruber, has her own stories to tell. Generally she asks one of the bartenders to stick around while she goes downstairs to the cellar to make sure everything is in order before shutting down for the night. One evening, she heard what she took to be a deep male voice call, "Debbie." It was faint, but clear. She thought it was the bartender, especially when she heard it again. Looking around, she found no one there with her, so she went upstairs to ask the bartender if he had called her. He said he hadn't. She went back down and decided to just start talking to whoever had spoken to her, and that seemed to silence it.

Another time when she was downstairs, she thought she saw someone walk by the door of the room where she was working, but when she checked, no one was there. It seems that the spirits from the hotel's past just like being there. And why not? The atmosphere in this restaurant is warm and inviting, the entertainment fun, and the clientele lively. Spirits can't partake of the food, but if they could, they would probably invite some of their friends from the other side.

THE OLD FLAT IRON

In response to our request, Charles Erb sent a story that had happened to him at a place that at the time was called Rosemary's, but is now generally known to locals as the Old Flat Iron. "It's at the point in West Bethlehem across from Bennet Toyota," he explained, "where Bethlehem starts and Allentown ends."

It began when he met a woman at this bar named Vandy.

"She said she was only in town for a while," he recalled, "and would then be off to a job modeling; she did not know where. Yet she did frequent this particular bar every Wednesday, so we got to talking and hit it off, if only as friends. She had no interest in anything more but said she wanted to listen to my poetry. Being a ham in that respect, I was more than happy to take her up on an invitation to go to where she was living and read a few poems for her. She said an old woman lived at the house and was letting her stay for a while. She gave me an address on the west side of Bethlehem, not far from the bar. I showed up around 8:00 P.M. the next night and found the house."

Vandy opened the door and invited him in, showing him around. "The odd thing was," he recalled, "there were no pictures or mirrors in the home and no trace of any old woman to speak of. The night went on and she seemed strangely detached from everything except my poetry, which she paid attention to. After a while, I decided I may as well leave because, frankly, nothing more was going to happen. I made my excuses and left."

But he remained curious about this woman, so the next day, he went back over to try and find her. He thought he remembered where the house was, but he drove up and down the street, checking and rechecking the number without locating the place. "There was no house at that address, as there had been the night before. The house, and Vandy, were gone as if they had never existed in the first place. And she never came back to the bar."

STEMIE'S

Easton once had a tavern known as the Black Horse Inn, which dated back to the 1700s. It was a stagecoach stop and a way-station for people coming up or going down the Delaware River. There's even a rumor that George Washington once visited. (Hey, where *didn't* this guy go?)

However, the ghost is much more modern, says current owner and manager, Al Stempo. (The place is now a family restaurant called Stemie's.) He told me the story, describing a few of the incidents that have happened since he and his wife, Maria, purchased the place in 2002.

A brave soul, Al already knew about the ghost before entering the deal. The former owner had described to him how pictures would fall off their hooks or fly across the room, how waitresses often tripped, dropping their plates, and how things often turned up missing. That didn't sound so bad to Al. He didn't believe in ghosts and he was eager to start his business.

So on a cold February 1, Al went to the building around seven in the morning to do some work. As he walked into the place, unheated because the electricity was not yet on, he challenged the ghost (just in case): "If you're here," he said, "then if you leave me alone, I'll leave you alone. But if you bother me, I'll get a priest in here to get rid of you." No one bothered him that day.

The restaurant is located at 831 South Delaware Drive and the story attached to it is this: in July 1928, during the gangster era, a man named Johnny Ferrara, associated with organized crime, would come there. One story has it that he kept money in the building, another that he was messing with the boss's wife. In any event, he was on the phone in the hall when someone came in and shot him. It was a hit, pure and simple, and as Johnny fell down the steps to the cellar, the perpetrator melted into the night. A beer delivery man found the body, says Al.

Although an investigation ensued and a suspect was arrested and brought to trial, no one was ever convicted for "Johnny the Wop's" murder. Perhaps that's why his ghost hangs around. Al claims that throughout the renovations, every worker he hired complained at one time or another of spooky things going on—pipes that knocked back when tapped, tools being moved, items missing. And several people have seen outright apparitions.

A couple came in one evening and as they were talking with Al, the man took two steps forward and nodded his head. His wife asked why and he said he was letting "the man" get by. She told him there was no man, but he described the person: dark hair, about five-foot-seven, a ruddy complexion, and wearing khaki pants. It wasn't so far off the mark for the dead gangster. Another customer once informed Al that a man was waiting in the other room for him, but when he went to check, no one was there.

Other incidents have occurred as well. Once someone put a bread knife down in the kitchen after using it and it suddenly flew across the room. A patron laid down a dollar bill on the bar and watched it slide a foot away from him, and a female customer claimed to see a man's foot from under the stall door in the ladies' room. She accused Al of being in there, but he was innocent. Indeed, the ghost seems to have no preference, since a man saw the image of another man in the men's room mirror, turned around, but saw no one there.

One day, Al kept dropping bread off the rack, so in good humor, he yelled at the ghost to quit, and directly thereafter came the sound of heavy footsteps going up the stairs. Al has also heard footsteps in the hall upstairs when he and Maria stay there overnight. Maria often hears her name being called out, but she says that she and the ghost get along just fine, because they're both Italian. However, "Johnny" apparently did not take as well to the former owner, who claimed she had no end of trouble.

In fact, Al had to admit that one incident that happened since he's owned the place was a little more serious. The phone went out during the winter of 2006–07 and the company sent over a repairman. Al took him into the basement and, as they were talking, Al joked about the ghost. It didn't seem to faze the man, so Al went back upstairs. About ten minutes went by and the repairman came running up the steps, asking to use the phone to call his wife. Al noticed that his hair seemed to be standing on end and he was sweating profusely. When the man's wife arrived, he insisted on being taken to the hospital. Al says that this man never revealed what had happened in the cellar and they never saw him again.

KING GEORGE INN

Another inn operating since the 1750s is the King George Tavern on Cedar Crest and Hamilton Boulevards in Allentown. It's on the register of National Historic Sites. Built in 1756, to be exact, it has a long tradition of serving travelers on the stagecoach route and has even helped protect against Indian attacks. When the American Revolution began, the area to the rear served as a staging ground for young soldiers drilling to fight for their country. Citizens also used the place as a town hall, church, courthouse, and the place to get news and social gossip. With six dining areas and three antique cocktail bars, it's one of the most well-known eating establishments in the Lehigh Valley.

As is often the case, lore about paranormal activity arises from a story involving a former employee. The basement area was once a dirt-floor storage place where employees would go to fetch things. One evening during the 1940s, a young dishwasher went down to wash out some of the table linens. Somehow, the lights went off and she apparently panicked. She stayed down there far too long, which alarmed other members of the staff, so they went to find her. To their surprise, she was hunched up in a corner, weeping profusely. When they asked what was wrong, she kept talking nonsense. They managed to make out that she had heard a baby crying and she was sure the sound had come from the cistern. Since there was no baby in the well, one staff member decided that the frightened employee might have heard a ghost. He researched the matter and discovered an incident that had occurred during the eighteenth century that appeared to explain the frightening phenomenon.

During the French and Indian War, as the British occupied the area, the French sent their Native American allies to the settlements to terrorize residents and drive them away. These warriors thought nothing of killing women and children, including infants. While no act is definitely tied to the inn, the slaughter of infants may well explain the crying of a baby. Over the years, others have also heard this chilling sound in the cellar . In addition, an employee once encountered a transparent, bearded apparition dressed in old-fashioned clothing who seemed to be laughing, but no sound issued from his mouth.

OTHER DESTINATIONS

We heard about several restaurants within ghosting distance of Bethlehem that reputedly host a specter, but since they're pretty far from our main focus, I'll just mentioned them here, in case readers wish to check out these places on their own.

- The Widow Brown's in Stockertown—haunted by the victim of a hanging, a ghost they call "Marvin."
- The Buckeye Tavern, 3741 Brookside Road in Macungie, west of Allentown, offers strange noises at night while staff are cleaning up. Sometimes they smell bacon cooking in the basement, where food used to be prepared. The building dates back to 1735.
- Applebee's, once Casey's Nightclub, at Catasauqua Road and Route 22, was supposedly built on a site where Indians attacked white settlers. The sound of a baby crying and a woman screaming are the reported phenomena.
- Magnolia's Vineyard Restaurant, 2204 Old Village in Orefield, once a hotel on the stagecoach line, has a ghost dating back to the Civil War: a female pining for a lost love who never returned. She shows up where an orchard once stood and vanishes when approached.
- The Inn at Maple Grove just outside Alburtis was established in 1783. On its menu is described the tale of a Native American once hanged in the Common Room, as well as a story about a guest who was murdered on the second floor. Among other spooky occurrences, phantom footfalls can be heard on the stairs.

RANDOM SPIRITS

Ghosts almost always like theaters, hotels, and restaurants, but we found other forms of enterprises that seemed to attract spirits as well. A colleague of mine, who once worked in the Allentown General Hospital at Chew and 17th Streets, told me stories that circulated there of a ghost called "the Conductor." Apparently, this entity is associated with a patient who was a former railroad conductor. Sometimes, when a nurse was transporting a patient in the elevator, there were persistent odd noises in the shaft. They began to believe the building was haunted and they'd warn one another to beware of the Conductor.

I was unable to find out just why this patient was the origin of these tales.

Another ghostly presence that acquired a name, "Micah," appeared on a property in Foglesville that once had been a fresh air camp for kids from the inner city. The person who now resides there, Bill, told me that he'd cleaned out some closets and found an old polio brace for a child. He came to believe that the ghost he'd experienced there had once been a physically disabled child—but one who could now run, because that's how some of the strange noises sounded.

Bill described one incident in which he had set out some cookies on a tray, and when he looked at them again, they had been stacked up in neat piles, but no one in the house had done it. He'd also find things missing that would turn up in other places. Once he put a book down next to the bed before going to sleep and then found it downstairs the next day. Bill always left his car keys in the car, but one morning he found them in the living room. No one else had used his car. He has no doubt that he is living in a haunted house.

But not everyone accepts such circumstances. In fact, some of these places are known as stigmatized properties.

STIGMATIZED PROPERTIES

A stigmatized property is a place where something occurred that could psychologically affect the buyer's decision to make the purchase. It could be a crime committed there, a death from an infectious disease, a suicide, or even a ghost. For example, the Chicago home where a federal judge's husband and mother were murdered sold for $140,000 below its listing price, more than fifteen percent off its worth, in a hot market. In another example, the person who purchased the house in Fresno, California, where Scott Peterson might have killed his wife had the house on the market for five months without an offer and finally accepted a ten percent loss.

"It's a beautiful house in a really desirable area," the realtor said, "It's really too bad that it has the stigma it does."

More striking was the 9,000 square foot luxury estate on more than 3 acres in San Diego where 39 members of Heaven's Gate committed suicide in 1997. Two years after the incident, a developer purchased the property for less than half the price at which it had listed ($1.6 million) prior to the mass suicide.

Closer to home, in Salisbury Township, not far from South Bethlehem, two brothers killed their parents and younger brother in a fit of rage over growing tension about house rules. It was such a violent crime that it brought reporters from as far as New York and Washington, D.C., so its notoriety clung to it for a while. While people in the Lehigh Valley still talk about this crime, which happened over a decade ago, few know where the property is. But after the murder, it was difficult to unload the home.

It doesn't have to be a crime that gives buyers doubts. A church for sale in Freemansburg got two offers, but the realtor had neglected to inform the buyers of one detail: it came with 600 graves. Not only that, unused plots were deeded to other churches and private citizens, and could be used at any time. Both deals fell through in a hurry. It was one thing to live next to a cemetery, but quite another to "own" the dead.

Some homes, too, have a reputation for being haunted, perhaps just because they resemble a house in a creepy Hollywood film or because they're run-down or the lawn is overly weedy. So-called spirit-possessed houses can be tough to move and some actually do have a spooky story attached.

On a Web site for Lehigh Valley Information, a list of ghost stories contains several from realtors, one of whom would buy stigmatized properties because he didn't believe in ghosts and they were generally good deals. However, when he moved with his wife into a particular house in Whitehall, north of Allentown, he changed his tune. Lights would turn on and off by themselves, despite rewiring them, and one day, the couple found all their bottles of medication pulled out of the cabinet where they'd placed them, and all the toys out of the toy box.

In the same area, a mortgage broker lived in a house where, after he had used dishes and left them on the counter, he'd find them placed back into the cabinets —still dirty! This happened every day, no matter how many locks he put on the doors. He even had friends come over to witness it, and just as he said, the dishes left out on counters were placed into the cupboards as soon as people left the room. (We wondered why he didn't set up a camera in the kitchen to capture this phenomenon.)

REALTOR'S NIGHTMARE

Every realtor knows the nightmare of having to show a property where something terrible has happened. The National Association of Realtors actually assists its members with stigmatized properties. In some states, if a property is alleged to be haunted the seller must disclose this fact. For example, California law states that disclosure must be made for up to three years after an incident occurred, and the state realtors' association there advises disclosing any such incident if a seller specifically asks.

In a New York case, the court allowed purchasers to back out of a deal when they learned that the property was reputed to have ghosts.

In 1990, a couple made an offer on Helen Ackley's Victorian mansion on the Hudson River in Nyack, New York. Buyers Jeffrey and Patrice Stambovsky made a down payment of $32,500 on the asking price of $650,000. The Stambovskys were unaware that the house had a reputation for being haunted until a local architect told them. In fact, it turned out that Mrs. Ackley herself had actively promoted the building as a haunted spot, with spirits in the attic and poltergeists in the pantry and garage. She had described the three spirits she lived with for several publications and had been featured in a haunted house walking tour. Supposedly, one spirit was a naval figure from the Revolutionary War, another was an elderly man that levitated, and the third was a woman in red who floated down the staircase. Ackley described them as gracious and thoughtful, and only occasionally frightening, but she took delight in their residence. Eventually, Ackley decided to move to Florida, so she put the house on the market.

While Jeffrey seemed undisturbed about the home's supposed history, his wife was less intrigued. She wanted to back out of the deal and have their deposit returned. However, Ackley refused to cancel the sale. She claimed they had agreed to purchase the home "as is."

Thus, the case ended up in court, with the Stambovskys claiming they were the victims of fraud. The court didn't agree, saying it had been their responsibility to learn about the home prior to making a financial commitment. Unhappy about that, the Stambovskys appealed the decision to the Appellate Division of the State Supreme Court and got satisfaction. In a 3–2 decision, the court decided in their favor.

The decision was written in *Stambovsky vs. Ackley*, in effect, saying: "While I agree with the Supreme Court that the real estate broker, as agent for the seller, is under no duty to disclose to a potential buyer the phantasmal reputation of the premises and that, in his pursuit of a legal remedy for fraudulent misrepresentation against the seller, plaintiff hasn't a ghost of a chance, I am nevertheless moved by the spirit of equity to allow the buyer to seek rescission of the contract of sale and recovery of his down payment." Justice Rubin, writing for the majority opinion, stated that Ackley "had deliberately fostered the belief that her home was possessed by ghosts," and should have disclosed this to any potential buyer. "Not being a 'local,'" Rubin added, "plaintiff could not readily learn that the home he had contracted to purchase is haunted."

This was a precedent-setting decision, with unusual implications. The obvious difficulty with making the determination whether a house is haunted goes well beyond having a home inspector look into the matter. However, the court failed to address such practical concerns. The only real issue for them was the effect on the property's value. If a property was reputed to be haunted, it could inspire negative opinions from locals but also attract ghost hunters from other places, who might take pictures and trespass on an owner's privacy. Since Ackley had promoted the home in national media, this possibility influenced the court's decision.

"Whether the source of the spectral apparitions seen by defendant seller are parapsychic or psychogenic," Justice Rubin wrote, "having reported their presence in both a national publication and the local press, defendant is estopped to deny their existence, and, as a matter of law, the house is haunted."

Some realtors think that keeping such things a secret only adds to the fear; buyers wonder why it was concealed and may fear there's more that's not being said. It's better to be honest. In thirty-four states, including Pennsylvania, any issue that could devalue the property must be disclosed, in particular a crime. Apparently a home in which a murder occurred is the most difficult type of property to sell. That problem would be magnified if several murders took place at different times —as if the property might have a curse or some kind of negative energy associated with it. A home in which someone committed suicide is second on the list of problems for realtors. The trick is to disclose the unpleasant facts without losing an interested client—which is no small feat.

Not in Pennsylvania, but well known, is the four-bedroom Brentwood home where Nicole Brown Simpson and Ronald Goldman were murdered in 1995. When put up for sale in the glamorous area the year after the double homicide, the asking price was $795,000. No one made an offer, so this prestigious property in an upscale neighborhood sat on the market for over two years.

In the meantime, ghost hunters made plans for investigations and rumors arose that the property was haunted. One claim, posted on the Web, was that sounds of a woman screaming had occurred in the condo *before* the murder (as if in ghostly anticipation), and afterward, people taking photographs found images that resembled both of the victims, especially in the tree leaves. The home finally sold for $595,000, far below the area's assessed value.

Yet even when such homes sell for close to the asking price, they tend to stay on the market for much longer than other homes. Only after the incident recedes in people's memory does a sale becomes more viable.

And not everyone will avoid stigmatized properties; some people actually hope to move into a home that comes with a ghost. However, they generally prefer a benign spirit said to watch over the place. The fact is, most alleged hauntings are just that: noises, odors, footsteps, or a quick glimpse of something that makes no impact on the living.

However, we did find a house for sale where the owners had experienced numerous incidents that would probably make any potential buyer have second thoughts. In the interest of their privacy, we will not post the address, except to say that it was on a main street of a town in the Lehigh Valley.

WAKING THE DEAD

This couple, whom we'll call Tom and Sally Jones, wanted to buy a home. They looked at one property, which they found to be immaculate and quite nice, but they nevertheless got the creeps from it, so they declined to make an offer. They subsequently learned that it had once been a mortuary. Eventually they found a lovely Victorian mansion for sale, and though they noticed a few odd things about it before they made an offer, it did not dissuade them. They would have reason to be sorry.

The stately house dates back to 1905, and two successive physicians had used it as their home and place of business. In those days, that meant making their own pharmaceuticals and doing surgeries. It's possible that patients died there, although the records on that are unclear. We do know that the second physician died there quite suddenly. It then came into the hands of his son, who lived in the home until it fell into disrepair. He'd allegedly had an altercation with his mother one day and a struggle ensued. The mother fell down the back staircase, situated off the kitchen, and broke her hip. Taken to the hospital, she suffered from her injuries for a few days before finally dying.

Sally and Tom learned about the house in 2002, when its contents were being prepared for auction. Taking photographs, they found unusual anomalies in two of them. Framed in the mirror of an antique throne chair on the main floor, for example, was the image of a man. The same was true in a photograph, taken outside, of an upstairs bowed window: this man stood there looking down at them. However, the house had been empty at the time. The realtor who'd shown them around dismissed the images as those of another customer who was probably looking at the place, but some time later they saw a photo of a previous owner of their home—the second doctor. They were certain it was the same man they had seen in the mirror and window.

This kind of thing was nothing new to Tom. In a previous marriage, he and his wife had lived in a one-room school house on a large piece of property in another area in Pennsylvania. In this place they could hear the voices of children. One day, a sink hole opened up and the building began crumbling into it. Having sufficient acreage to rebuild elsewhere on the property, the family moved out and watched their former home slowly come apart, to the point where it had to be demolished. But they continued to see and hear things associated with it: most often was the sound of children playing, but there were images of people out in the field as well.

For the most part, this did not bother them, but one incident did. Tom was in bed and his wife was in another room. He woke up to see what appeared to be two formless black shapes emerge from the floor and move toward him. He began to shake and believed that something was trying to pull him off the bed. His wife came in and thought he was having a seizure. But the incident stopped as suddenly as it had begun, and they never knew what to make of it. Still, it bothered them.

They invited a psychic over who claimed to be able to tell them all about the property. She held a séance, inviting other people to participate. She began by going into a trance, rolling her eyes back, and naming names; she also spoke in other voices. Tom was generally bored, but he grew more interested when this woman gave each attendee readings about themselves. They all swore (says Tom) that the information was valid. In addition, many of them claimed to "see" someone they knew who was deceased—and not always someone they wanted to see. Yet as far as the house was concerned, at first nothing much happened. The psychic invited them into a circle, and soon thereafter a sound occurred, like a baseball bat rolling down the steps. Tom looked around but never found the object or the source of this noise.

To Tom's disappointment, the psychic was unable to explain the black shadows that had come at him; even worse, she predicted that he and his wife would break up, and soon, that prediction came true. (That's not hard to spot for someone experienced in observing people, as most psychics are, but Tom was impressed.) Tom then married Sally and ended up in what seemed to be yet another haunted property. He wasn't happy about that.

Sally liked the home immediately upon entering the foyer through the front porch.

She saw that a second front entrance led to a former patient waiting room (now a sitting room), with original woodwork and colorful stained glass. Unique sliding panel doors opened to a former treatment room, which the Joneses hoped to turn into a dining room. They also wanted to create a kitchen from a room once used to store bottles of medicine.

They made an offer, which was accepted, and as soon as they moved in, they experienced unusual activity. For example, the Joneses came home one evening to find a large painting that they'd hung in their sitting room on the floor. When they examined the hanging pins, more than adequate for the job, they found that all had been sheared straight off, as if by a knife. Sally found it exciting, as she'd never seen anything like this before, but Tom wasn't as pleased. He told us that whenever he came home from work, it sounded to him as if there were hundreds of people talking. He also began to see what looked like the residue from bare feet going across the hardwood floor in the kitchen. They were moist, as if someone had walked through water or was sweating.

Sally's 28-year-old son also had some negative experiences. The first one occurred when he was doing laundry in the basement. He looked up to see a dark mist float down the stairs towards him. As he stood watching, it stopped in front of him and took the form of a man, who commenced to wave his arms over his head, as if in a state of urgency, and to shout. The trouble was, no words were audible. This figure reminded the young man of his recently deceased father, and despite his fear, he was curious to know if his dad had something important to tell him. But when the figure reached toward him beseechingly, he'd had enough. He left his clothes and high-tailed it up the stairs. After that day, he'd never enter the basement alone again. But it didn't matter, because he had several more encounters in other parts of the house.

In his bedroom one day, he came home to find all the dressers flipped over and his clothing strewn about. This upset him greatly. Then as he was walking down the back staircase—the same one on which a woman had taken a fatal fall—he felt a rock pelt him in the back. He turned to see who had thrown it so hard. With several step-siblings, it could have been any of them, but when he looked up, no one was there. He then remembered that he was home alone. He sensed that some unseen presence had thrown it and thought perhaps whatever was in the house was specifically targeting him. After that, he moved out and would not come to the house again without family members present. He was convinced the place was haunted with a malignant entity.

The animals in the home—a cat and Gordon retriever—were bothered as well and would avoid certain rooms. Sometimes the retriever seemed to be looking at something no one could see and he would often wake up growling, though he was otherwise a mild-tempered dog. He was startled awake one night, along with Tom and Sally, from the noise of a heavy object rolling down the stairs. The retriever barked in warning, as if someone was there, but when Tom went to check, he could find nothing that would have made such a sound. Everyone was in bed.

Different members of the family reported seeing flitting images of someone crossing a room, but it was often too quick to even make out if it was a male or female, although occasionally someone would spot the figure of a young girl. They were all convinced there was more than one entity in the house. Objects would disappear and reappear in odd places, and they learned to get used to this.

Indeed, there may have been patients who'd once been in the home. Tom described a large man who had twice come into the bedroom, grabbed his leg and said, "Can you help me find my foot?"

"Whatever it is," he said, "it feels wronged. They don't belong here. They're not evil, but they know they don't belong here and they don't want to be here."

Among other problems was the typical issue with things being moved from one place to another and the sense of the presence of someone who was not visible, but who seemed to be hovering. In addition, they often heard things falling down the back staircase—where the woman had fallen to her death. And as they took photographs of the house one day, a cat appeared in pictures taken in the basement, although no cat was present and it was not the family's cat.

The worst incident, also reported by Tom, occurred about four years into their stay. He worked a night shift and had gone to bed one afternoon to take a nap. Normally the dog joined him, but on this day the retriever refused to come in. Tom could hear his daughter going from her bedroom to the bathroom, and as he drifted off, he heard the disturbingly familiar noise of many voices speaking at once. Suddenly, he sensed something near. The sheets began to ripple, like a flag in the breeze, and the movement soon gained speed and intensity. He knew that his own legs were not causing this. Then he felt as if something had entered him and was getting him to reach over toward the position where his wife would be if she'd been with him. He had lost control of his body and it was acting under someone else's command. He felt the bed shake and heard a male voice cry, "Please help!" It grew louder and louder, and he felt helpless to do anything. He was certain his daughter could hear the voice and would come rushing in, but she did not. The voice seemed to be coming from him, although he was not willing the words himself.

He had no idea how long it continued, but finally the sheets relaxed and the experience diminished, leaving Tom exhausted. He felt physically beaten up, inside and out. It had been one of the worst experiences of his life, and when he was able, he got up and checked with his daughter. She had not heard anything. Deeply disturbed, he left the house, with the intention of never coming back inside. He'd felt so many emotions during the experience, ranging from anger to shame to love, and even intense sorrow, as if many different entities had passed through him.

"They were looking for help," he later said, "but not from me." From work he called Sally to tell her about it, stating that he was not coming back. But she told him the house was quiet and persuaded him to come home. He remained uneasy there, and insisted they sell the place. They'd already talked about this, but now they called a realtor. Tom was adamant.

Although the house went on the market and was beautifully maintained, over the course of three months they had no offers. In fact, not one person even came to see it, not even after they took part in a historic house tour in which 500 people had shuffled through. Sally believed it was because they were supposed to stay there. The activity, which had increased since the tour, intrigued her and she was ambivalent about selling. However, she did agree to call in a person to spiritually cleanse the house. Tom continued to press to get rid of it and did not wish to consider the possibility that, despite his earlier experiences, the entity or entities might be attracted to him. Since there were no previous owners to ask about similar experiences in this house, they did not know whether selling it would end their encounters.

That was the last we heard from them.

SO, WHAT IS A GHOST?

In the *Introduction to Ghosting* chapter, we mentioned the 1972 experiment in Toronto in which a group of eight people conjured up a ghost they named Philip, getting results, from knocking on a table to seeing the table dramatically move. Their experience tends to confirm the notion that people who want to see ghosts probably send out energy and somehow make it occur—a sort of telepathic psychokinesis.

In fact in 1974 another group did something similar with a "collective hallucination" they named Lillith. She, too, received a tragic history, and she made noises for them much quicker than Philip had for his group. One evening, the two groups converged to enjoy the attentions of their respective entities. One source states they ended up interviewing Santa Claus.

One might assume, then, that all ghostly phenomena are psychological in nature. In fact, the human brain is powered by electricity, so it wouldn't be surprising if it was indeed the basis for phantom incidents. The brain sends impulses into the body to make our muscles and digestive systems work, etc., so why not into the atmosphere as well? Certainly, some scientists accept this notion.

In 2006, an article was published in *Nature* about how Swiss neuroscientists had stimulated an area of a female patient's brain, inducing the same effects people claimed to feel in haunted spaces. The subject was twenty-two and lacking in a history of psychiatric disorders or delusions. During their examination of her prior to surgery for epilepsy, they stimulated the left junction of her temporo-parietal lobe. She quickly said she had an impression of someone standing behind her, but no one was there. She described him as young, silent, and posing in a way to mirror her position.

The doctors urged her to sit up and they stimulated her brain once again. This time she said he had wrapped his arms around her, just like the way she had her arms around her knees.

Then for another test, she held a card in her right hand, and after stimulation in the same area, she again reported the shadow person, but this time she had an impression of what he wanted. "He wants to take the card," she said. "He doesn't want me to read."

The doctors believed that with this discovery, they had explained away the supernatural; it's all in the brain.

But had they? Perhaps all they did was stumble across an area in the brain that responds when phantom entities are present. Nothing they said actually undermined the paranormal. In fact, they'd done their experiments on an unimpressively small subject pool—one—and her experience hardly mirrored all the types of things that millions of people around the world have reported. Again, this theory falls short of explaining all the phenomena. It's interesting, but it doesn't go far enough.

In the UK, other researchers were determined to prove that ghosts were all in the mind and they tested a much larger number of participants. They took groups of people to reputedly haunted spots, asked them to describe their experiences and prior knowledge about the place, and then concluded that the experience of ghosts was the result of environmental cues. Those spots did consistently inspire creepy feelings, even in people with no prior knowledge about the ghost stories associated with them. Thus, the researchers concluded, they must be responding to what a place looked like—perhaps a stereotypical creepiness. The psychologists went on to surmise that mediums who can correctly identify a haunted place, though they aren't familiar with it, are more sensitive than others to such visual cues.

The main problem with this study, as we see it, is that the researchers neither identified the environmental factors nor proved them to be causal. They'd already dismissed ghosts before they even started and thus found support for their theory. But that's not only easy, it's the opposite of science. Anyone can prove a hypothesis; it's the disproving of a hypothesis that gets difficult.

Even so, we can't dismiss the work that's been done with infrasound, i.e., sound at a frequency too low to be detected by the human ear (about 16 or 17 hertz). Infrasonic waves have been studied since the 1960s, when a French scientist noticed sound waves that hurt his ears and shook his lab, but could not be identified as noise. In fact, infrasound provides the early warning signals for weather events such as tornados.

Infrasound, while not detected, nevertheless can cause sensations of fear and awe. It could explain the vague uneasiness that people feel when they think some unseen presence is nearby. In a 2003 experiment, infrasonic elements were introduced into a concert and concert-goers were asked to rate various pieces of music. Those pieces that included infrasonic aspects, unbeknown to the listeners, invariably induced descriptions of anxiety, uneasiness, sorrow, revulsion, and even fear. A few reported getting chills down their spines. If infrasonic waves are present in certain areas, those areas might gain a reputation for being haunted, in virtue of the unexplained experiences they produce.

The late Vic Tandy, a computer specialist-turned-paranormal-debunker, believed that a frequency of 19 hertz was responsible for "ghostly phenomena." Supposedly in his lab in a reputedly haunted building in Britain he suddenly felt uneasy, started to sweat, and thought he saw something gray out of the corner of his eye that had certain human properties. But nothing was there. Then, when an item he was working on began to vibrate despite being gripped in a vise, he traced the activity to a fan emitting a sound wave frequency of almost 19 hertz—the conditions under which a human eyeball will resonate. He believed it had produced both the vibration and his optical illusion. He wrote papers indicating that infrasound was at the heart of most of the renowned hauntings in places around Britain.

Still, infrasound doesn't quite get at all the phenomena we've explored here. For sure, some is the result of superstition, but if infrasound were entirely to blame, then everyone in a place should experience uneasiness and illusions. That doesn't happen. And with a phantom that different people who don't know each other can see, well, it seems that nearly everyone who's in those rooms (or wherever) should then see it, not just a few. Tandy is to be commended for trying to figure it out rather than just assuming that a ghost was coming for him, but he hasn't convincingly explained it all, either.

In fact, other physicists have questioned Tandy's theory. Those who work with infrasound have gotten results such as uneasiness, fatigue, and pressure in the eyes and ears, but not hallucinations.

With this debate in mind, let's look at the results of a similar experiment before we offer an idea about the nature of a ghost.

Three experienced psychical researchers came together for a period of two years to investigate the activities of the Scole group, in Scole Norfolk, in the UK. This group of people—three middle-aged couples—had claimed to be meeting with spirit guides that had produced a range of phenomena. Among the activities were tape recordings of voices, spontaneous images in undeveloped film, objects appearing out of thin air (apports), shadowy figures, moving furniture, and even sophisticated messages from renowned but deceased scientists. They produced communications from these spirits in several languages, and the investigators looked for evidence in every way they could conceive to prove that deception or fraud was taking place. They were unable to do so. The Scole Report was published in 1999, stirring great controversy.

In essence, the investigators pondered the question of just what counts as acceptable evidence of the paranormal. The Scole group had started up in 1994, meeting in a dark cellar at the home of the group's leader and one husband/wife team served as the mediums through which the "guides" communicated. Points of light appeared and darted about the room, responding to spoken requests. Via the mediums, these spirits offered information and could be questioned and even cross-examined, so it was clear to the scientists that information had not been prepared beforehand.

However, at one point after the report was published and new experiments were devised, the spirits asked the group to cease meeting and the activity vanished. The members were dismayed.

To some extent, the investigators were rightly criticized by colleagues for not having adequate safeguards in place against deception, but the Scole investigators argued in return that no amount of deception could account for the wide variety of phenomena they had witnessed over the two-year period—especially when they were interacting with spirits on highly technical subjects. They could also see no motive for fraud.

The Scole group had no desire for fame or gain, and some insisted on anonymity when the report was published; their stated motive had been to explore mediumship for a new age. While no profound messages were forthcoming, as some critics expect from the Other Side, there's no reason to believe that the psychology after death is anything but continuous with the psychology of life. Why *should* ghosts know amazing new things beyond the grasp of mere mortals? The fact is, said the investigators, the Scole group did produce information not otherwise available to them, but known by the deceased that allegedly showed up at the séances. This was not an induced "Philip phenomenon," but an attempt to provide a way for entities we view as ghosts to communicate if they so desired.

Whether or not the results from Scole are convincing, they certainly provide material for skeptics and believers alike, both of whom will work to prove their own positions on the subject. Will we ever have an answer? I don't know. Do we want one? I'm not sure.

My own theory, for what it's worth, is fully detailed in *Ghost*, but here's a basic framework, based on the large collection of manifestations I've heard or read about. I can't prove it, but philosophically, it makes sense to me:

Consciousness, reason, and emotion are components of the mind.

When a person is physically alive, the mind and body form an inter-related unit, each part operating via a specific type of information-based energy.

When consciousness leaves the body, it retains a residual body-awareness based in this energy, which resembles a memory.

Body awareness fades unless certain patterns of emotional encoding from the mind/body connection anchor it to the body or some other form of information-based energy.

Consciousness then becomes like a phantom limb, i.e., echoes of a former personality or ghostly phenomena, and the body memory becomes part of a memory field (which some physicists believe can exist independent of a brain).

In other words, a "ghost" might be a residual memory, with different degrees of intensity, awareness, and sophistication: perhaps a noise, perhaps an apparition, perhaps a voice communication.

Whatever it is, Dana and I believe that the potential for authentic hauntings is more interesting to explore than to dismiss, so we continued. Let's expand our range of haunted places for the final part of our narrative.

WITHIN GHOSTING DISTANCE

Over in Hellertown, off exit 67 on I-78, walks "der Ausleger," a phantom undertaker who liked to steal bodies. This story derives from the nineteenth century, just as the earliest undertakers were being utilized. For assistance with burials, townspeople looked to men who owned businesses in carpentry and furniture making, because they already made the coffins. Putting activities once done by family into the hands of others had a distancing effect that probably accounts for the Ausleger legend. One version holds that the area's early settlers, father and son team Christopher and Simon Heller, would help with burials and became a bit too eager for the task. One or the other of them became der Ausleger. Another account shows this entity as a man paying an eternal price for robbing the graves of Native Americans.

So, this ghostly (ghastly) undertaker roamed around Lower Saucon, visiting families where someone had died to assist with washing the body, digging the grave, and driving the death wagon. He might even remove the "death water" that was used for corpse cleansing. In fact, mourners soon learned not to pour the death water down a hole on their property, because it would attract him to those spots. Thus grew the ritual of taking it to the cemetery to discard. (That's possibly why some people think that cemeteries are haunted—because der Ausleger is skulking around the little pools of death water.) A pair of run-down gray steeds pulled his wagon, and people claimed to have seen it from Phillipsburg to Easton to Hellertown.

A living undertaker was traveling along Springtown Road, his team pulling his hearse. Der Ausleger drove up behind, startling him, and he took off. But he couldn't lose the fiend. They raced together along the road until finally der Ausleger and his horses just up and disappeared. Afterward, the living undertaker had stories to tell. One wonders if he changed his profession.

It gets more gruesome when we learn that der Ausleger was seen robbing graves and that he'd sometimes show up prematurely, before a person had died. Apparently, he wasn't attentive to protocol. Supposedly, you could hinder der Ausleger from disturbing a grave if you buried certain documents (*Laadpapers*) with the body

—a birth certificate, a *Himmelsbrief* (heavenly letter), or a pow wow charm. No one knows what he did with the bodies once he had them.

Der Ausleger might also appear at funeral dinners, which back then were often great feasts. He'd help himself to some funeral pie, made out of meat or raisins. In fact, people say that he still attends such functions to this day, though the pickings are much diminished. He's not there to cause any harm, apparently. He just mingles with the living as a reminder of what we can all eventually expect. You'll be able to spot him because he looks just slightly out of place.

Like der Ausleger, the Lehigh Valley covers a lot of ground, and while this book is largely about Bethlehem proper, a few places close by merit attention as well. We received numerous reports about spirit activity from many parts of the Lehigh Valley, but we tended to focus on tales with a substantial context or some peculiar quirk.

GIRL IN THE GRAVEYARD

There's a cemetery in Trexlertown, to the south of Allentown, which is the location for a rendition of a rather famous urban tale. During the 1940s, the story goes, a young woman lived across the street from Resurrection Cemetery. (We assume they mean the Resurrection Cemetery on North Krocks Road above Route 222; the address for that is actually Allentown, but it's in the general area of Trexlertown.)

Anyway, she contracted tuberculosis, weakened, and died. Her loving family buried her in her best dress—one she'd worn to parties. Not long afterward, people claimed to see a young, well-dressed girl wandering alone along the road right by the cemetery. When travelers slowed down, she'd ask for a ride. Since it was usually late at night when this occurred and she was out there alone, they often obliged, and she'd climb into the back seat. But once they reached the place where the cemetery ended, she'd disappear.

Just about every state has a version of this tale, but Chicago claims to be the originator, with the woman being buried in a cemetery there—also, it turns out, called Resurrection Cemetery. In fact, she's referred to as Resurrection Mary. In that tale, the girl also loves to dance, but she appears to be much more aggressive about getting a ride, to the point during the 1930s of jumping onto the car's running board before disappearing. Over the decades, this tale shifted and eventually the telling involved young men who would meet a mysterious blue-eyed blond at a dance and take her home. Upon getting to the address she gave, it turned out to be the cemetery and when the man turned to question her, the girl would be gone. Some versions add that he'd give her his jacket to wear because she was cold, and he'd then find it the next day, folded neatly on top of a grave that had her name on the headstone. She, too, had been buried in a party dress.

Next, let's look at one of the more reprehensible stories about this area, which takes us into neighboring Bucks County, because the incident figures into some of our narratives.

THE BIG CHEAT

In a park in Salisbury Township that borders the Lehigh River, I came across a sign that mentions the Walking Purchase of 1737. In this infamous episode of shameful behavior on the part of the white man, it seems a deal was struck with the Lenni Lenape Indians, part of the Algonquin Nation, who viewed a large area of land in Pennsylvania as their hunting ground. However, the King of England thought it belonged to him, so he'd parceled it out to certain favored subjects.

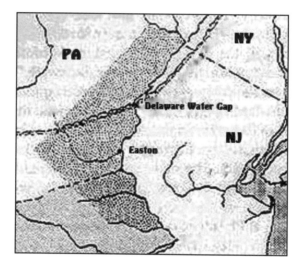

Dark Area is Boundary of the "Walking Purchase"

William Penn, one of the earliest settlers, had a reputation for dealing fairly with those who were here before him, and he'd already made a number of purchases along the Delaware. But then he returned to England, dying there and leaving his sons and other agents to carry on his affairs. Debts came due, so these men wanted to sell land to raise funds, as well as to position themselves for better trade options. Unfortunately for the Lenape, the land on which these men set their eye was where Lenape villages were established

Two of the Penn brothers apparently didn't take after their father's ethical code. They came up with a questionable scheme, showing Chief Nutimus (or Nootamis) a "copy" of an unsigned deed to the land they coveted (mistakenly believing he spoke for the whole tribe). Originating from earlier times—1686—the deed was supposedly in accord with the wishes of the Lenape ancestors. The Penns falsely claimed it was a binding contract, with terms stating that they were to be deeded the amount of land that could be covered by walking for a day and a half.

The deed itself was not only a lie, but the scheme involved a shrewd ploy to convey the image of a leisurely walk that might cover about twenty miles along the Delaware River. That seemed reasonable to the Lenape, and wishing to honor their ancestors' promise to William Penn, they agreed.

However, the true plan involved hiring three strong and athletic runners to cover as much distance as they could in the designated amount of time. The Penns had marked out and cleared the area well past the Forks of the Delaware, engaging men for a trial run to ensure the acquisition.

On the appointed day, September 19, the Lenape arrived at Wrightstown to oversee the "walk" and accompany the agents, as they'd often done with William Penn, but they quickly learned that they'd been fooled. The runners took off at a quick pace, going all day and into the next. The Lenape who went with them had to drop out—as did two of the runners. But one of them, Edward Marshall, managed to cover sixty-five miles, getting into and past the Lehigh Valley to Blue Mountain, north of Mauch Chunk (now Jim Thorpe). From his achievement, the Penns acquired about 1,200 square miles in northeastern Pennsylvania. But they (and the white settlers) lost some friends, via political quarrels with the Lenape that continued for several decades.

Chief Lappawinsoe, one of the four who had been part of the accord, was angered over the transaction, stating that the agents for the pact "should have walkt along by the River Delaware or the next Indian path to it... should have walkt for a few Miles and then have sat down and smoakt a Pipe, and now and then have shot a Squirrel, and not have kept up the Run, Run all day." His repeated protests and formal appeals fell on deaf ears, as did those of other chiefs. The King of England eventually authorized an investigation, but nothing much came of it.

The Lenape were people of their word, so they eventually turned over the deed for all this property. But they soon learned that if they didn't own the land (a concept unfamiliar to them), they had no rights to fish or hunt there. It's little wonder that Native American tribes in the area, inspired by agents from France, came to view white settlers as a threat.

In fact, Edward Marshall lived down the Delaware, at Smithtown, but for a few years he moved to a farm close to Easton. His family was nervous that the Indians might attack in retaliation for his part in the Walking Purchase. When he was away one day, that's just what happened. Mrs Marshall locked herself in the house while her children fled to hide. The Indians broke down the door, grabbing her and killing her. In a subsequent attack, they killed Marshall's son as well. He then moved his surviving children back to Smithtown. While some Smithtown residents have claimed that the ghost of Mrs. Marshall walks the river banks looking for her husband, it's more likely that if she's a restless soul, she's wandering around the farm where she suffered.

At any rate, white settlers arrived and created towns and townships in the area. One of the earliest ghost stories we discovered took place in Salisbury Township.

THE DEVIL CLAIMS A SOUL

In 1753, residents in one area of the Lehigh Valley requested to form a township and the court granted it. Thus was born Salisbury Township. I soon learned from Reverend Gary Piatt of the Jerusalem Western Salisbury Church, that Western Salisbury was created when Emmaus and Allentown cut some parcels from the township. Fountain Hill took more. Apparently, the township was supposed to have been called Salzburg, to refer back to the magnificent Salzburg, Austria, but some confusion between English and German produced *Salisbury*.

In a book about the township's history, I learned about fieldstone markers for Native American graves in the Western Salisbury churchyard. Of course, the peace-loving Lenni Lenape were on the land before white men showed up, having villages of several hundred scattered around the area. A museum not far from the church provides some history. But I was more interested in a tale from the other Salisbury Township, because it's one of the original ghost stories from here.

Inn of the Falcon

Since we started with the sign in Salisbury about the infamous Walking Purchase, let's have dinner at one of the restaurants there. The Inn of the Falcon, an impressive colonial stone tavern, is situated at the intersection of Emmaus Avenue, Susquehanna Street and Seidersville Road, near Fountain Hill. Known for its excellent food and atmosphere, it's a busy place, with limited hours, so if you want to check it out, be sure to call ahead. *(Note: at press time, the inn was in negotiation for a change of ownership and name to Bolete.)*

While dining there, we talked with Shirlee Neumeyer, one of the owners, and she gave us a framed article about the inn, from the *Globe Times* (now the *Express-Times*), dated 1980: "Acker Hotel has a New Look and an Old Ghost Story."

In sum, the reporter on this story described the following: Long known as the Acker Hotel, the Inn of the Falcon was once a log cabin on one of the first grants made by the Penns in 1735. During the Revolutionary War, it was a way-station for travelers. By 1809, with the erection of a stone building, the site became a stagecoach stop. One of the squatters on this parcel of land was in fact Solomon Jennings, who'd participated in the Walking Purchase (and was the first to drop out, going only eighteen miles). Peter Acher was the first tavern master, and although the inn's ownership changed hands more than a dozen times, it retained the name Acker. The place became somewhat infamous when the body of a female murder victim was discovered in the parking lot across the street. But that's not the incident that led to the ghost story.

Albert and Shirlee Neumeyer purchased the structure on May 18, 1981, to restore it, opening it as a restaurant of quality the following year. It has remained warm and tasteful for over a quarter of a century. The restaurant's main claim to fame, according to the Neumeyers, was its connection with an eighteenth century episode that was immortalized in a poem, "The Legend of Tambour Yokel," by Joseph Henry Dubbs, found in the book *A History of Lehigh County, Pennsylvania*—perhaps the poem's 1876 edition written by William Egle. A member of the clergy, Dubbs was born in North Whitehall, Pennsylvania, in 1838. After holding various pastorates in the German Reformed Church, in 1875 he became a professor of history and archaeology at Franklin and Marshall College. Doing research, he discovered many documents relating to the history of the German churches in Pennsylvania. The poem he published is about a man who tangled with the Devil.

Supposedly, this man, Tambour Yokel, had an association with another man; some say they were drinking buddies who often got into good-natured fights, but the poem indicates they were actually "ancient enemies." Yokel went off to war to be a drummer boy, and when he returned, he was raring for a fight. But his former foe, he learned, was dead. He was disappointed, as he wanted to knock someone about.

Yokel, being already a "worthless wretch," reportedly became even more predatory. As the poem goes, some people whispered that during the war he'd "learned but arts of a bird of prey" and had apparently made a deal with the Devil to "save his life."

Back at home, Yokel discovered that his enemy was buried in a local churchyard, now the cemetery associated with the Old Jerusalem Church in Salisbury Township. After drinking for a while, he decided that it mattered little if the man was alive or dead; he still wanted to fight.

> *"Ho! What of that?" The drummer cried*
> *"Perhaps it is well the coward died;*
> *But I know a way, as you'll see to-night*
> *To bring the man from his grave to fight."*
> *Then a dreadful oath the ruffian swore,*
> *He would call him forth to fight once more.*

So his comrades continued to drink with him, awaiting the promised moment and wondering what Yokel was up to. Apparently, he drew out the suspense, finding excuses not to go, because they finally mocked him and urged him to prove what he'd claimed he would do. "Ho wizard," they cried, "Why don't you go/To the churchyard now to meet your foe?"

Not to be humiliated, he cursed them and went out the door. He marched straight to the cemetery, which was at least a mile away, down Emmaus Avenue and up the hill on Church Road. He was probably quite drunk and was ready to put on a show to prove himself.

"Come forth!" he cried, through the startled night,

"Come forth, thou fiend, from the grave and fight!"

As he reached the gate to the cemetery, he shouted his challenge once more. In the dark, he could barely see the neat lines of rounded stone monuments. He certainly could not have read the inscriptions to find the grave he wanted. (Dana and I tried it on a cold, moonlit night and couldn't tell.) He waited, and no one knows whether he hoped for action or silence. Certainly his jeering comrades offered no help, as no one actually accompanied him to the dark burial ground. Alcohol may inspire a bit of pseudo-courage at times, but not that night.

Salisbury Cemetery

The wretched Tambour Yokel did indeed get an answer. Apparently, he'd awoken a supernatural force, and in light of the deal he'd made during the war, that's not generally a good idea. His comrades, awaiting his return, realized that something was amiss.

> *"But soon a cry that was wild and shrill*
> *Was heard from the churchyard on the hill.*
> *'Help, help!' he cried, but none drew near,*
> *His comrades trembled, aghast with fear,*
> *In silence waiting, - that godless crew*
> *While cries still fainter and fainter grew."*

Apparently, rather than run to see what had happened, they waited out the night. Nothing more was heard. They figured that Yokel would soon return to the inn to tell them he'd staged an elaborate hoax.

But Yokel never returned. Only by sun's light did anyone learn what had become of him.

> *"There mid the graves, the man they found*
> *Naked and cold on the trodden ground:*
> *Scattered his garments, far and wide;*
> *Bloody the soil where the wretch had died."*

Something had clearly come in the night and ripped into this braggart. The brutality ensured that the story would last, even to this day.

> *"Did a panther perchance of the forest tear*
> *The limbs of the wretched boaster there?*
> *Or was it the fiend, as the neighbors say,*
> *That bore his godless soul away?*
> *Ah! None can tell, - nor cared to know*
> *But a mighty hand had laid him low.*
> *Yet, with a shudder, men still relate*
> *The tale of Tambour Yokel's fate;*
> *And none forgets the legend grim—*
> *How a fearful judgment was sent to him."*

Apparently, thereafter, people avoided that cemetery, just in case. Whether panther, ghost, or Satan himself had done the deed, no one was willing to clarify what might have occurred that night, nor risk it for themselves. In fact, the church's congregation declined thereafter, and the historian attributes it to the legendary incident. "That this legend powerfully affected the community cannot be gainsaid," the book insists, "for even today the story is widely circulated and frequently credited, and there are still people to be found who will drive several miles extra on a dark night to avoid passing the cemetery." The congregation was finally reorganized in 1847 and a new church built.

Even today, the small cemetery has a spooky, melancholic appearance, perhaps because many of the headstones are so old.

But the Inn of the Falcon, too, has its own incidents. Occasional bartender Carolyn Berhard said she believed she'd seen a white form one day out of the corner of her eye as she glanced at a mirror while getting supplies in the room upstairs. She thought it was female. If there's a ghost of Tambour Yokel, it could be associated with either the inn or the cemetery, as spirits often seek to haunt the places they emotionally frequented—places that have meaning for them. The inn, or stagecoach stop, was the last place he'd felt safe—and brave.

HOUSEHOLD ENTITIES

Also in the general area, we heard about a couple of haunted houses. Since they're private homes, we won't give out the addresses, but several incidents have been noted in both in recent years. In the first home, we'll let the current homeowner tell it:

"When I purchased the house, the former owners told me that they'd sometimes felt the distinct sense of someone in a first floor bedroom and the adjacent bathroom. I made that bedroom into an office and used the one across from the bathroom as a guest room, while I took the room upstairs.

"The house felt quite friendly inside and I was happy to be there. I had a few strange dreams within a month of purchasing it involving people in the room with me, but I always dismissed them as my imaginings. Then a friend stayed with me, going to bed in the guest room. In the morning she told me that she'd heard a male voice say two words. She didn't know what the words had been, but the voice had been distinctly male and it had been in my upstairs room. I assured her that no one was there. Nor had I turned on the television.

"Two months later, my parents were staying in the guest room, and on the second morning, my father said, 'I see that you were up late working last night.'

"I shook my head. 'I went to bed at 11.'

"He seemed puzzled. He explained that he'd gotten up around two or three o'clock to use the bathroom and had looked in my office. 'I saw you sitting in the chair in front of the computer. You were looking at the screen.'

"Surprised, I again shook my head. 'Was the screen on?'

"He thought about that and said, 'I don't think it was, but I could see you there. Your hair was braided.'

"I looked at him. 'It wasn't me,' I said. 'I don't braid my hair and I wasn't up working.'

"He went pale. 'I've seen you twice,' he said, 'Both nights.' He wanted to know if there was a hotel nearby to which he could move. Instead, I persuaded him to stay another night and look again. To his credit, he did. In the morning, he told me that no one was in the chair and there was nothing in the room that looked like a person, so he hadn't mistaken a coat or some other item for 'me.' The third night had not been like the two preceding it.

"Since this was the same area of the home where the former owners had experienced something, I thought it was interesting, especially because Native Americans had lived in the area. Hence, the braided hair. The house itself was not very old—and in fact, its builder had died in a tragic accident—but the land could host any number of entities.

"And there was one more thing. I was on the deck one night, talking with a friend. The light was on inside, illuminating that hallway, and my friend was facing it. Suddenly he looked startled. I asked what was wrong.

"'I think I just saw someone move fast across the hall!' He described it as a dark shape, flitting so quick he couldn't say exactly, but all of his senses had gone on alert, as if it were a real person. It had been the size of a person.

"But there was no one inside. Another guest saw a dark shape the size of a person move through the guest room. A psychic told me there's definitely a female presence here and she's curious about my work. I tend to think, since different people have experienced things in the same general area, there's something there. He or she or they never bother me, except perhaps to move something from one location to another, but I hope one day I'll get to experience an incident myself. Still, I haven't yet slept overnight in the guest room. I've thought about it, but I'd rather let others tell me what they see. I think I'll just stay in my own room."

The other private home was a Greek Revival house, built in 1880. The owner, whom we'll call Joan, told me that once, right after Halloween, a neighbor greeted her and then said, "I see you had a big party yesterday." This was a puzzling remark, because she hadn't. The neighbor went on to say that she'd seen three men wearing cloaks and top hats on the porch. She had figured it was a costume party.

Inside the house there were more such incidents. One day when her children were little, Joan was upstairs and one of her kids came running up to say, "You have to come down! The man in the dining room wants to talk to you." She described him as glowing and white, with a beard. But when they went down, no one was there.

More dramatic, during the 1970s there were times when they could see a procession of Native Americans walk through their living room. They'd move diagonally across, as if keeping to their path from earlier times. Sometimes they were transparent, other times seemingly solid. In fact, every once in a while, Joan said, "you could only see part, like a child's hair or a travois."

On one occasion, she was taking a nap and when she woke up, she saw a man with slicked-back hair standing in her bedroom. He wore a pin-stripe suit, buttoned high, with a small lapel and wide stripes. He smiled at her, then disappeared.

71

As it turns out, the home was built on the site of an Indian massacre. It appeared to attract other types of spirits as well.

So let's move on.

A Ghost Who Doesn't Like Change

The place where Route 378 meets Highway 309 offers a tale about which few people are aware. George Motter approached us after we'd presented a "Body Bag Lunch" radio show at DeSales University. We had told our audience that we were seeking ghost stories and he had a good one involving his father's former property nearby.

There once was a grist mill at that spot on Highway 309, which had a gruesome story associated with it. The former owner, a man named Jacob, had a tragic accident. He fell into the mill and came out as grist, going straight into the nearby creek. After his remains were recovered and buried, he apparently decided to return in another form. The mill was sold, coming into George's grandfather's hands. When George's father was a kid, he'd go up to the mill's top floor, which was always freezing cold, no matter how hot it was outside. He noticed that his dog would never follow him to that area. Some experts on spiritual matters came to the mill, George said, to affirm that there was a spirit in the place. They could not say whether it was "Jacob."

Most intriguing is what happened when the county planners decided to create the 378/309 connection. The grist mill had to go, they decided, so they tore it down. Things got interesting when they tried to move the creek, said George, so they could lay down the road. Each day they'd rechannel the water, and the next day they'd return to find it flowing along its original course. They did this over and over, and finally gave up. The road was rerouted and the creek left in its original spot. Apparently, that's the way Jacob wanted it.

Ghosts At School

Not far from the grist mill location, along Station Avenue, is DeSales University. In existence for over forty years, it has a top-rated theater program that's in high demand. In fact, I'm told, two ghosts hang out in Labuda, the building for the Department of the Performing and Fine Arts. Who they are is anyone's guess, but some believe that one is a former professor who's not keen to leave. Students have also reported seeing a child wandering about the arena stage area, or crying backstage. Some, working late in the building, have described the sound of heavy footsteps and doors closing when no one was about.

The Shakespeare House

A good walk away is the two-story stone house that became the Jacquier Center, also dubbed the Shakespeare House, because it's where the offices are situated for the famed Pennsylvania Summer Shakespeare Festival (PSSF). Reportedly, the ghost of a woman dressed in a fashion from a past century has been spotted after hours on the porch. In October 2004, the following facts were published in the university's official calendar memo:

Lisa Higgins, the director for marketing and public relations for the PSSF, has experienced some unusual incidents. During the 1995–96 season, she returned from lunch one afternoon and went into her temporary office on the first floor. She heard someone say, "Hello," followed by the rather distinct sound of footsteps on the wooden floor upstairs. Since there was construction going on, she assumed it was one of the workers, but no one answered her call. Upon looking outside, she realized that the workers' truck was not parked in the lot. That meant she was in the building alone…save for a seemingly benign spirit. "It was so distinct and so sustained," she recalls. She'd been certain someone was there.

Her next experience occurred over a weekend. She had a few hours of work to do, so she took her daughter, Mattea, with her. Mattea went wandering around. A co-worker had brought in doughnuts and placed them on top of the cupboard. When Mattea returned, Lisa told her she could have one.

"The nice lady in the kitchen already told me I could," she responded. In fact, this figure had even shown her where they were. But no one else was there, and certainly no one in the kitchen.

Then a general manager heard someone say "hello" three times, and he was told by others who worked in the building about the appearance of a woman in a long dress, gliding through a room. Someone also reported the sensation of being flicked repeatedly in the ear by an unseen hand.

The staff refer to this entity as "Mrs. Brown," in reference to a woman who once had lived in the house. Constructed in the 1800s, it had been part of a farmstead. When it went with the land on which DeSales was built, it served different purposes, from housing the administrative offices to being a residence and dining hall. It's been headquarters for the PSSF for over a decade.

In 2004, TV/Film Director Scott Paul had a group of students go in with me on the night of a lunar eclipse to see if we could film anything. We set up an infrared video camera in the attic (a place that Lisa said gives her the creeps), and the students were excited to get quite a lot of orb activity on film. In my opinion, it was mostly dust, but I didn't spoil their fun.

We then went over to the Department of Social Sciences in the Tucker House, where my own office is located, and set up a camera. We got a few lone orbs flying across one room, which were a little less ambiguous than those at the Jacquier Center. In fact, at Tucker House, we've often joked about our ghost, since it's the oldest building on campus, but in truth, I've spent many evenings there alone and nothing has ever disturbed me. But then, I've never spent an entire night.

ART OF DARKNESS

Easton, Pennsylvania, appears to be a veritable portal for spirit activity, or maybe the residents there just get into their ghosts. They even offer a ghost walk during the Halloween season. I spoke with Alicia Rambo, whose mother is involved with the Scarecrow Festival that occurs on the third Saturday in October in the historic downtown area. As part of this festival, they offer two nights of ghost stories. Last year, they also held contests for scary hair, scarecrow building, and carving cool jack-o'-lanterns. The ghost tour takes place in the evenings, and anyone under eighteen must have their parents' permission to attend. It must be scary, as it's not advisable for kids. Reportedly, this tour draws well over a hundred people, so get your tickets early at the Farmers' Market.

One day Dana and I ventured over to Easton, about eight miles east of Bethlehem, to check out a few of the hauntings there.

Our first stop was the impressive Historic Easton Cemetery at 401 North Seventh Street. Initiated in 1849 by Dr. Traill Green, who saw how the local churchyards were filling up, this site was actually considered back then to be "in the country." Incorporated that year, the cemetery began with forty-three acres and has grown to nearly one hundred. A booklet states that more than 29,000 people have been buried here, with the first one laid to rest on All Saint's Day, November 1, 1849. The vision that inspired it was based in the idea of preserving a place not far from town where people could go, not just to visit the graves of their loved ones and tend the plot, but also to make it a social gathering.

Historic Easton Cemetery

Despite the reputation cemeteries have today of being creepy, during the nineteenth century the local graveyards were *the* place to socialize and rejuvenate, and with good reason. Many were developed for precisely these results and became cultural and community centers. The more luxurious bone yards were known as garden cemeteries.

Père-Lachaise in Paris was the world's first to be designed specifically to merge nature with art to lure the public into the sanctuary of the dead. The final abode of Balzac, Oscar Wilde, Victor Hugo, and Jim Morrison, the extensive landscaping inspired many sculptors to display their talents. Tourists came in droves and artists whose work might otherwise have not been noticed soon found themselves in demand. This decorative necropolis quickly inspired American entrepreneurs.

In 1831, the seventy-two acre Mount Auburn was laid out near Boston on land clothed in diverse botanical life. By far the largest American burial ground created to date, it was to be a tastefully ornamented arboretum. The word, *cemetery*, which means "sleeping chamber," came into widespread use and plot-owners were expected to provide the finest memorials within their means. The monuments were as much a display for the enjoyment of others as a way to show respect for the dead.

To achieve the twin goals of selling space and "taming" nature, the Mount Auburn planners joined forces with the horticultural society. Unlike the neglected city graveyards, these plots received perpetual care. Thus was created a garden of graves that defied gloom, uplifted spirits, and offered recreation.

The idea caught on and spread. Green-Wood in Brooklyn (which inspired Central Park) and Laurel Hill on Philadelphia's Schuylkill River followed a similar plan. These magnificent parks soon became popular leisure destinations, inviting city folk back to nature. On any given weekend, crowds gathered to picnic, share gossip, and increase their aesthetic awareness. In 1860 alone, 140,000 visitors passed through Laurel Hill's seventy-four acres.

The rural cemeteries affirmed hope and eclipsed the fear of death. Headstones, monuments, and elaborate mausoleums emphasized resurrection. Ornamentation was key as stone carvers imitated the grand sculptures of Europe. Egyptian, Gothic, and Grecian representations of eternity's threshold provided regular diversion for Sunday promenades. Laurel Hill, bordering Fairmont Park, eventually held over 33,000 monuments, many of them stunningly detailed. For touring Europeans, a trip to these places was high on their "to do" list.

Yet over the years, enthusiasm waned. The cities encroached and the neglected cemeteries spoke more of mortality than eternity. Strictly speaking, they became places not for the living but the dead.

Easton Cemetery appears to have been inspired by the concept of the garden cemetery. It's a well-treed, lovely place to walk on any part of the nine miles of paved roads—at least in the daylight. We heard that a "white lady" wanders the grounds after dark, but no one is certain who she is or why she's there. I'm aware that a murder victim was found on the grounds in 1996: a thirteen-year-old girl who was tortured and killed over a bad drug deal had been dumped into an old storage vault. However, some people who know about this figure in white think it's "Mammy" Morgan.

MAMMY

Easton Library

An area near Interstate 78 was settled around 1725, growing within three decades to a township of 150. John Williams was one of the more prominent settlers, so the area became Williams Township. One of the highest points is Morgan Hill, named after Elizabeth Bell Morgan, aka "Mammy." Her husband had died from yellow fever, contracted when they lived in Philadelphia, and one source says she used his medical texts to assist with the epidemic in Easton. (Another source claims he was a lawyer and she thus used his law books to assist people with legal transactions.) Elizabeth opened a public house, or hotel, on the hill. Her nurturing ways earned her the affectionate title, Mammy.

One of her beloved pieces of furniture, a tall clock, can be seen at the museum run by the Northampton County Historical and Genealogical Society (NCHGS), which we'll get to in a moment, but Mammy is more closely associated with the Easton Library at Sixth and Church Streets, not far from the cemetery. In fact, several spirits are associated with this building, and for good reason.

After getting a grant from philanthropist Andrew Carnegie, the library building committee looked around for land and decided that the best possible spot would be the city's oldest burial ground, now defunct. It was overgrown with brush and most of the families had long since died or moved away. The residents had to be transferred to a new area… or at least, the stones had to be moved. (People in those days did not have the benefit of movie theaters to inform them of the consequences, a la *Poltergeist*, when one moves the headstones but leaves the bodies.)

Mammy's Grave

At any rate, digging commenced and the workers found one grave after another —to the tune of 514. During this excavation period, phantom lights were spotted in the general vicinity. Those surviving relations who were located were able to claim their ancestors and move them, but not all of the dead had a surviving relative in the area. According to several sources, thirty bodies were unclaimed, as were some bones and disarticulated body parts, so these were dumped together into a concrete vault that's under the present-day parking lot. It's likely that some remains were never recovered.

The bones of two prominent citizens, Mammy Morgan and William Parsons, were reburied there on the grounds, with markers to honor their deeds. Mammy's are on the library's west lawn, but apparently her spirit wasn't keen about being disturbed. Members of the library staff have stories to tell about the place and some believe that the ghosts of misplaced souls wander about the building, moving books, turning on lights, and generating strange noises. Officially, no one affirms a "haunting," but when no one's listening, some have told me about locked doors that open and close by themselves, drawers that open by some invisible force, and books that suddenly fly off the shelves. A few people claim they've been touched when no one was there.

Indeed, passers-by have reported white figures looking out the windows at night, especially on the second floor.

Taking Care Of Business

Several people told us about a story first published in 1851, called "The Fate of a Flirt of the Olden Time," and it refers to a notorious incident in Easton. To track it down, we went to the NCHGS building on South Fourth Street and met with director Colleen Lavdar. She was kind enough to describe several unusual incidents in that building and to provide us with a copy of the story of the flirt.

A socially prominent woman and American writer, Mrs. Elizabeth F. Ellet, published the account in *Godey's Lady's Book*, and it was later published in a historical account of the Valley. In 1948, a curious Easton resident, Mrs. William Hay, looked into the facts behind the story, and while she could not document them, it appeared that Mrs. Ellet had not qualified the work as fiction. Thus, it was more likely true. Supposedly Mrs. Ellet had heard it when she visited Easton.

This event apparently took place when Easton was just a small settlement, surrounded by "primeval woods." Residents tended to keep to themselves and not travel to such disturbing places as Philadelphia. They weren't keen about change of any kind, so the arrival of strangers created quite a stir. One day, they learned that someone was moving to the area—an Englishman and his family—and everyone was quite curious about what they would be like. They were dismayed to see furniture arrive to the family's still-empty home that was more flamboyant than they preferred, and the yards being prepared in a way that defied their generally grim and religious frame of mind. (Obviously, this story can't end well.) The house was located on North Fourth Street, where the offices of the Express-Times are currently located.

Finally, the family arrived—a man, a woman, and a seven-year-old boy. It turned out that the Englishman, "Mr. Winton," was a jovial, outspoken fellow, a member of the Colonial Assembly, who'd brought his family "to rusticate for a season" on the Delaware. They'd lived among the wealthy in cities like Paris and Philadelphia, so they were clearly much more sophisticated—and social—than the longtime residents of Easton.

And there was a problem, which cropped up quickly: these people did not attend church. Not only that, the stunningly beautiful wife with the long black hair, perfect figure, and flowing skirts seemed to lack appropriate modesty. Her eyes were sharp and joyful, and she laughed too easily. "In short, she appeared to the untutored judgment of the dames of the village, decidedly wanting in reserve." However, the men liked looking at her. They began offering their services, inspiring jealousy from the other women. Even worse, Mrs. Winton had a servant to do her chores and did not follow proper protocol for social engagements. Yet attempts at ostracism failed to have any effect, as Mrs. Winton seemed to find plenty of company in male admirers.

In October, she and her son went riding into the forest. When a bird startled the horse, a man appeared to grab the reins and steady it. He'd not yet made the woman's acquaintance, but she used her charm to engage his attention. She then invited him to visit her, which he did. Quite a lot, it turns out, and the neighbors noticed. In fact, they now observed that Mrs. Winton was quite the coquette, apparently determined to win the admiration of all the men in town—even the married ones. "She flirted desperately with one after another, contriving to flatter each one that he was the happy individual especially favored by her smiles."

Then Mr. Winton left for the winter to attend the assembly meetings, and the flirt was left to tend the home fires on her own—much to the delight of many a man who thought he now had an opportunity to move in on her. She became the object of much gossip and disapproval, and it seemed clear that she would come to a bad end. The women of the town passed around rumors that she must be consorting with spirits and engaging in witchcraft to make men bend so easily to her will.

They were determined to reveal her for the witch she was, so they took to spying on her. This paid off when they saw her go with a man into the woods. The women called a meeting and then in the dead of night, they donned black masks and went looking for the Englishwoman and her supposed supernatural consort. They grabbed her from her house, binding and gagging her, and in the presence of her pleading son, dragged her into the woods. In a pond, they dunked her over and over as retribution for stealing the attention of their husbands. Then they left her on the bank and returned to their own homes.

The next day, Mrs. Winton's body was found by the pond. Apparently, she'd died there. An investigation got under way, but the perpetrators kept a conspiratorial silence, and no one was arrested for the murder. Popular opinion seemed to indicate that the victim had been punished for witchcraft, and death was just an unfortunate side-effect. Despite their religious beliefs about the serious nature of murder, the matter was not vigorously pursued.

But apparently Mrs. Winton was not keen about her killers going free, as rumors arose that after her death, she showed up at the pond. Even after the pond was drained and the area developed (now Bank and Church Streets), she continued to appear at the spot where she'd died. People who did not even know the story reported seeing a beautiful woman in an old-fashioned white gown. But then, perhaps she moved, as the sightings were reported in the area on Spring Garden, between Bank Street and North Fourth. That stretch is occupied by the First Presbyterian Church and the Churchman's Business School, part of Easton's Alvernia College.

I met with Reverend Chuck Holm at the First Presbyterian Church, which was undergoing renovations. He was eager to have this tale included and he proved to be a wealth of good information about local lore. While he's not seen the ghost himself, he's aware of the reported sightings on the building's front steps, the street in front of the church, in the former parsonage, and even inside the building (documented by Mrs. Hay). He showed me where elaborate gardens for the church had once been (now occupied by the business school's building), and then took me into the basement, where workmen had located what appeared to be tunnels for the Underground Railroad. He also gave me an article about the ghost from October 13, 2003, because it had an additional tidbit of information.

First Presbyterian Church

Reporter John A. Zukowski, for the Express-Times, did his own sleuthing on this story and found an intriguing connection with Edgar Allan Poe. Apparently, Mrs. Ellet sought the dark poet's attention, though he was married, vying with another female poet, also married. Ellet's rival, Frances Osgood, had long black hair, like Mrs. Winton, and Poe evidently enjoyed a literary flirtation with her —much to Ellet's annoyance. When the women got into what Zukowski calls a catfight, they used the written medium to debase one another, which inspired Zukwoski to ponder the possibility that the tale of a flirt was perhaps more symbolic than real.

So that's one of Easton's most enduring ghost stories—even referred to as "the ghost" of Easton—but there are others as well, and one is actually part of forensic history.

A ROPE, AN ISLAND, AND AN EXPERIMENT

Some of the staff at the NCHGS told us that things have happened inside the museum after hours to cause them to believe it's some type of paranormal activity. In fact, upstairs, Colleen twice saw an old-fashioned voting box turn completely on its own. No windows were open and no one was touching it.

One of the items Colleen showed us was a collection of pieces of rope used in executions-by-hanging. It was a pretty gruesome array, and the thinnest of them actually figures into a famous story from the area that produced two ghosts. Noting that a copy of the trial is in the library's collection, Colleen supplied the details of the incident.

Easton Historical Society

In the Delaware River is Getter's Island, with an upstream tip that nearly touches the Pennsylvania riverbank. It's named for Charles Goetter, now often spelled Getter, so we'll use that spelling. Getter was a German immigrant (hence the name, Goetter, which was more likely Götter). He was courting two women in 1833 and one of them, Margaret Lawall, claimed she was pregnant. Under pressure, Charles married her but apparently refused to live with her as man and wife, because he loved the other woman, Molly Hummer. In fact, he'd apparently once said, "I'll have Molly Hummer if I have to walk on pins to get her."

His wife was reportedly working as a maid on the estate of Peter Wagener, and shortly after their wedding Charles came one night to take her for a walk. She was wearing mostly black. The next morning, she was found dead, tossed over a stone wall into a quarry by Greenwood Avenue, and when her body was recovered and examined, it was clear to the doctor that she'd been strangled. Naturally, given Getter's anger toward this woman, he was the best suspect, so he was arrested. Yet he refused to confess to the deed, so preparations commenced for a trial. To defend him, Getter engaged the service of a famous and skillful Philadelphia lawyer, James Madison Porter.

Supposedly, a self-proclaimed psychic examined the corpse, because her "powers" allowed her to discern whether Getter, when he was brought in to look at it, was guilty or innocent. That wasn't much by way of evidence, but forensic science was barely even recognized in those days. Thus, to this story, I'm going to add one more character, because most people who tell me about the Getter incident do not know about this man's part in the proceedings. If not for him, the story would have ended entirely differently.

During the nineteenth century, American physicians had noticed that resolving criminal cases that garnered public interest could generate fame and advancement, like celebrity trials do now. In addition, these cases had proven a productive venue for demonstrating what the new medical science could do. To this point, only medicine and toxicology had made forensic advances, and doctors in America looked to noted figures in France, aspiring to acquire a similar reputation. One such American physician was Samuel Gross, who had taken an early course in medical jurisprudence in Philadelphia. Unable to develop a practice there, he'd returned to Easton, his hometown, and thus ended up on the side of the prosecution in the Getter case. Asked to do a postmortem examination on the victim, he was certain that Mrs. Getter had been strangled.

The trial commenced on August 19, 1833, and when Gross took the stand, Porter questioned his procedure for examination and analysis, then attacked him for failing to examine the woman's brain for signs of a cause of death other than strangulation. She could have died from apoplexy, he suggested. Given the incomplete nature of the examination, Porter wondered how could Gross be so certain about strangulation.

Undeterred, Gross described the research to date (mostly from the advanced medico-legal professionals in France) on signs of asphyxiation by strangulation. Indeed, he had done his own research by strangling and dissecting upwards of seventy dogs, cats, and rabbits to examine the damage done to the neck and throat. To his mind, that was more than most doctors would have done, and it was such clear proof of strangulation, he'd not had to look any further.

Porter brought in a dozen physicians during the weeklong trial to contradict young Gross, as they offered their own findings of apoplexy due to extreme stress, but Dr. Gross stood his ground, confident of the science involved. Juries in those days knew nothing about science, let alone forensic science, and they typically responded only to the logic of the circumstances. Clearly, a good logical case could be made against Getter, science or no science. After only thirty-six minutes of deliberations, the jury found him guilty. He still protested his innocence, but a date was set for his hanging. There were no long appeals processes in those days, so he knew he would die quite soon.

As the grim day approached, Getter confessed, affirming the analysis of Dr. Gross, who went on to acquire an impressive reputation in the medico-legal field. But Getter had a date with the gallows. The city took on a carnival atmosphere, Colleen told us, as people from around the countryside poured into town to see the event—perhaps 20,000–30,000. (In only a handful of years, newspapers would exploit a spectacle like this in a New York-based murder, creating yellow journalism, but that had not yet happened.)

Getter donned a white suit and was escorted into the streets by Sheriff Daniel Robb. A procession of people accompanied them along the half mile to the island in the Delaware, where the gallows had been constructed. At the shore, the killer had to cross over a series of boats strung together in a flotilla, as there was no bridge. People noticed that his manner was calm and collected. Quietly, he said good-bye.

Getter had requested to be hanged by a method different from the typical drop-and-break approach. He wanted to be drawn up and choked. So the rope was placed around his neck and then drawn up fast. But rather than break his neck, as it was supposed to do, the rope itself broke and the choking Getter fell to the ground. "That was good for nothing," he was quoted as saying.

He had to wait there, experiencing the pain of rope burn and contemplating his end for twenty-six minutes, before a second rope was brought, this one much stronger. To get on with it, he adjusted his scarf to hide the mark on his neck from his recent ordeal. He then waited for the rope to tighten again, and it did. As Getter was lifted off his feet, he struggled and kicked. By some accounts, it took him fully eleven minutes to die. The authorities left him hanging for half an hour, to be certain, before cutting him down.

People say that Getter's ghost walks around on this small island, perhaps due to the extra trauma he endured before dying.

His former wife is restless as well, it seems, and maybe she's unable to move on because she feels a little guilty. The tale came out afterward, says Colleen, that she'd been a mother before, so Getter might not have been the man who had made her pregnant. Perhaps she took advantage of him. In any event, they both died as a result.

Travel along William Penn Highway toward Bethlehem and you'll arrive at the Northampton County Country Club, the place that Margaret Getter reportedly haunts. She wears a long black dress and an equally black bonnet. People in Easton have told me that the club was built over the quarry where her body was found.

Supposedly, the old court house in downtown Easton is haunted as well, based on reports of noises that come from courtrooms when no one is in them. A jail nearby, where executions once took place, might be the source.

Getter's Island figured into another tragic tale not long after this trial. In 1860, the steamboat Alfred Thomas exploded after beaching against the protruding ground, killing at least ten passengers.

THE SHOW MUST GO ON

Like many towns around the world, Easton also claims a haunted theater. It's the State Theater at 453 Northampton Street. They even know the ghost's name —Fred, or Freddy. Among those who claim to have seen him are staff members, theater patrons, members of the Board of Directors, and people just walking by the building.

State Theater

It seems that from 1936 to 1965, a man named J. Fred Osterstock had been the manager of a company that had owned the theater. He'd even lived there, near the foyer, during 1955 when a horrendous flood, caused by two hurricanes, swept into town and made his house uninhabitable.

The ghost lore most common to theaters involves actors and actresses who cannot give up the limelight, as well as managers who love the venue. Occasionally, a theater reports a ghost, formerly a patron, who appears in the seats, but mostly the hauntings occur on stage or backstage.

The story of Freddy is posted on the State Theater's Web site, so they're not shy about sharing it. In sum, as people lost interest in live performances during

84

the 1970s, there were reports of mysterious occurrences. When the building was known to be empty, a man would be spotted in the back. He might be standing still or walking into a closet. Despite exhaustive investigations, no one was ever found. (Perhaps, like the Phantom of the Opera in Paris, he had access to secret doorways that led to deep, dark cellars where no one dared venture.) Someone who saw a figure walk off the stage one night and vanish said he looked like a picture of Fred. That's how the ghost acquired his name.

He's probably the only ghost to have an annual award ceremony named for him. The Freddy Awards honor outstanding achievements among high school students.

* * * * * * * * *

And, so, we close our tome of titillating tales, hoping we have offered the area a solid account of both history and mystery. From hitchhikers to ladies in white to phantom singers and undertakers, we've been intrigued by the variety of ghostly lore in this former Moravian settlement. It's likely that there are many more such stories to be uncovered and brought to light, and we will continue to collect and explore.

BIBLIOGRAPHY AND RESOURCES

Adams, Charles. *Ghost Stories of the Lehigh Valley*. Reading, PA: Exeter House Books, 1993.

Benert, Richard. "The Moravian Book Shop since 1745" (pamphlet).

Boyer, Dennis. *Once Upon a Hex*. Oregon, WI: Badger Books, 2004.

Eagle, William. *History of Lehigh County, Pennsylvania*. 1876.

Ellet, E. F. "The Fate of a Flirt of the Olden Time," *Godey's Lady's Book*, date unknown.

Fuller, John G. *The Ghost of Flight 401*. New York: Berkley, 1976.

_____. *The Ghost of 29 Megacycles*. New York: Signet, 1981.

Guiley, Rosemary E. *The Encyclopedia of Ghosts and Spirits*. New York: Facts on File, 1992.

Hamilton, Kenneth G. *Church Street in Old Bethlehem*, Bethlehem, PA: The Moravian Congregation of Bethlehem, 1988.

Jeffrey, Adi-Kent.Thomas. *Ghosts in the Valley*. Southampton, PA: Hampton Publishing, 1971.

_____. *–More Ghosts in the Valley*. Southampton, PA: Hampton Publishing, 1973.

Nesbitt, Mark: *The Ghost Hunter's Field Guide: Gettysburg and Beyond*. Gettysburg, PA: Second Chance Publications, 2005.

Nesbitt, Mark and Patty Wilson. *Haunted Pennsylvania: Ghosts and Strange Phenomena of the Keystone State*. Mechanicsburg, PA: Stackpole Books, 2006.

Ramsland, Katherine. *Ghost: Investigating the Other Side*. NY: St. Martin's Press, 2001.

Smaby, Beverly Prior. *The Transformation of Moravian Bethlehem*, Philadelphia, PA: University of Pennsylvania Press, 1988.

Solomon, Grant and Jane. *The Scole Experiment: Scientific Evidence of Life after Death*. London: Piatkus, 1999.

Spencer, John, and Anne Spencer. *The Encyclopedia of Ghosts and Spirits*. London: Headline, 1992.

Zukowski, John. "Easton's Church Ghost Story: Tale Links beautiful Woman, Writer, and Place of Worship," *Express-Times*, October 31, 2003.

Katherine Ramsland has published 30 books and teaches forensic psychology at DeSales University. She has looked for ghosts since she was a kid, has collected ghostlore from around the world, and has actively tried to record ghostly manifestations over the past decade.

Dana DeVito manages the Moravian Book Shop in Bethlehem and has been involved in some of Katherine's ghost expeditions. She is also a forensic nurse.

Other Books by Katherine Ramsland:

Ghost: Investigating the Other Side
Cemetery Stories
The Heat Seekers
The Blood Hunters
The Science of Vampires
Piercing the Darkness: Undercover with Vampires in America Today
The Forensic Science of CSI
The CSI Effect
Beating the Devil's Game
The Human Predator
The Vampire Companion
The Witches' Companion